The Things I Didn't Learn in Kindergarten

Brittany Lytle

blylte

ISBN: 0615999921
ISBN-13: 978-0615999920 (blytle)

To the (not-so-troubled) kids: The Littles
Each of you taught me so much. This is my attempt to give back to you a piece of what you gave me. A tribute of sorts. An incredibly small gift to show you how much you mean to me. I am changed, for the better, because of you.

To the Bigs.
Although I won't break it down specifically by person, situation, or story, you have gifted me with life lesson after life lesson. I will be forever grateful to have spent the most naked year of my life with you all. Thank you for doing the same.

To Adam.
Who loves me and walks with me. The way you love and care for me is beyond anything I deserve. The way you encourage me is cherish-able. I am forever and ever indebted to you. From the depths of my heart, with love.

To each of you reading.
May you find a bit of hope in the glimpses of my journey with these young people who, without trying, changed my life forever.

All the names of the Littles have been changed after much debate to protect their stories, but my deepest hope is that they would each understand how much good can come (has come) from small lessons they were unawarely teaching.

All of these memories are to the best of my recollection and are in no particular order. Regardless, they've grown me into the woman I am today.

THE THINGS I DIDN'T LEARN IN KINDERGARTEN

It started just like any other program I'd ever done. I was the able one: more capable, older, wiser, better off, and much more mature. I wasn't sure exactly what it was, but I knew I would teach them something.

Days went by. Weeks. Months. And eventually, the year. I still wasn't able to figure out what I'd taught them, but surely, I did. I had to believe I did.

It's as I sit here now--without them--that I am able to realize maybe the only thing I was able to teach was that they were much better teachers than I ever dreamed of being.

I guess I should explain what I'm rambling about before we go much further. The most educational year of my life (the year AFTER college) was spent at a discipleship training program partnered with a residential care facility for "at-risk" teenagers. It's a life-on-life approach at discipleship, spending much more time together than apart.

And of course, I dressed in pride (although my sweatpants may not have shown it), thought I could teach them something. How ludicrous; how bizarre!

The training period was not for me. I had come for the kids--I didn't need to be with the others doing the same job as I. The kids were my priority: *my coworkers, not so much. I had come to teach, and I was anxious to get to it.

Learning was never my forte--which is interesting considering how badly I wanted others to learn from me. But this year was a great paradigm shift for me, as I began to learn from those I'd come to teach.

*I learned very quickly, I needed my coworkers badly.

1 ASHLEIGH LOVED JASON

We all know that love is patient and kind. It is not self-seeking. It keeps no record of wrong. It does not envy or boast. It never fails.

Ashleigh loved Jason. And I have learned a lot about love from this young girl. Even when it hurt her, she loved him. Even when it was difficult, she loved him. Even when he needed more than just her, she loved him. Even when he wouldn't do the same, she loved him.

In the process of loving him, she wasn't able to love herself well. She had become too focused on pleasing another that she forgot to care for herself. I have a tendency to do this.

In the midst of being at this place, she began to work on identifying struggles, admitting things to herself, and reshaping her relationships with her parents. Through this process, she was able to see the way she did not love herself.

There were tears. There were many journal entries. There were self pep talks and breakdowns. She was trying to live with the person she'd become and love herself for the first time . . . in far too long.

Ashleigh knew the time had come. Jason could no longer be what he'd always been. She had to love him from a distance. Without words. Without touch. Because sometimes, love looks different.

She had begun to respect herself. She became more healthy. She stopped trying to impress. She was much more friendly. She began to love more people. She started letting others in, and for that, I am so grateful. Ashleigh loved well . . . even herself.

Walking alongside her, I realized how little I, too, loved myself and how much I needed to. Walking alongside me, she became such an encouragement in this process. I'm still on that journey. And so is Ashleigh. I believe it will be life-long. And we're okay with that.

Ashleigh taught me that love truly is beautiful. And we have both discovered how much greater it is when you love and are loved in return. In this area, she was my teacher, and I'm sure she doesn't know.

May·we love hard and well. May we love up close and personally unless from a distance is more loving. May we love ourselves and others so fully.

2 ROY WAS UNASHAMED

He was young, impressionable, and yearning for friends. Yearning so badly it almost hurt. Roy talked a lot. He was one of those kids you'd offer five dollars if he didn't talk for ten minutes. He told way-cool stories in an attempt to gain friends.

His sister was a model. He was in a gang. He'd done more drugs than he could remember, and he (at the age of fifteen) had already had and removed several tattoos.

Some of those things may have been true. Maybe even more than I believed. But I will say, there were no marks, scars, or any physical evidence that even one tattoo ever existed.

He wrote notes to girls to make them feel special, and ultimately to be liked. But his efforts went unnoticed-- actually, there were very noticed. Noticed and mocked.

For Roy, the mockery (though negative attention) was all he needed to keep it up. His stories continued, the notes progressed, and he measured his success by how much trouble he was in.

One of his proudest moments was when he got to be the lookout guy. A couple of other boys had stolen some over the counter medication and told Roy he could be the watchman. He did it. He even partook in the attempt to get high from the stolen meds.

You know, it was in that moment that Roy fit in. He was a part of something. For the first time, he had friends.

But not really. After the incident happened and the kids received their consequences, Roy was no longer cool. He was who he'd always been to them: the joke, the exaggeration.

It took a while, but Roy finally ralized that was not how friends treated one another. He began to be more real with the staff. He longed for someone to know him. Or at least, desire to know him.

Watching Roy, I learned we're all like that: desiring to be known so badly that we'll do almost anything. But I think it's the part where Roy became more vulnerable to staff and less showy to the kids that really hit me. Roy wanted to be known so much that he became real . . . even when it wasn't as cool, even if it seemed to belittle his character.

He'd gotten to a place of total depravity. And thus, my prayer for us all: to learn from Roy, just how wretched and dirty we are. But my hope is that we'd not go to that place to impress but instead because that is the people we are.

May·we embrace our realness, our wretchedness: in order to be known. To be a part of something. To be cared for in the most honest of ways.

3 SAME DATE BETH

My first half hour with her was spent walking around the basketball court, so she could watch him play. She opened up quickly, told me her life story, where she'd been, who she was, and all she aspired to be.

She asked me questions, listened as I answered, and giggled an awful lot. Finally, I realized she giggled when she made eye contact with this boy. She was fourteen, and her giddiness showed that!

I asked, "Beth, do you like that boy?" She said they were just friends, but it was her giggle that answered my question. They had come to the program on the same day.

They were the new kids. They didn't have to do it alone. For her, he was the other. As long as he was there, they could do it together.

It's funny, the things we do and why we like people. She had nothing in common with him . . . except a date on the calendar. And sometimes, that's all it takes.

He didn't return the crush, but he accepted her. Because for him, she was also the new kid. She was on his team. He thanked her by being friendly; she welcomed that thanks by flirting.

Her flirtation got less and less subtle. He finally told her he liked someone else. She tried to like others. But try as she might, they already shared something no one else could understand.

I guess when someone understands a way no one else can, something in you knows you've got to stick together. She could not do it alone. And neither can we.

May·we walk together as a team. May we choose to be helpful. And may we choose those that are helpful. May we leave no man behind. No man alone.

4 CHARLIE AND THE SIMPLE THINGS

I like music: jazz, R&B, rap, country, pop, hip hop, whatever's on the radio, really. I enjoy it. Sometimes, lyrics will float around in my head or tug on my heart strings, but music is like a treat, not a demand.

Charlie was funny, caring, a loyal friend, and compassionate. Now, these are things this soon-to-be-eighteen-year-old bad boy never wanted anyone to know, so he'd act the opposite. He'd curse, threaten, run, hit, and spit. Anything he could think of just to keep up this bad boy image.

Sometimes, in his forgetting to keep it up, he would do really great. Be back to the things he didn't want us to know. He'd be sweet, silly, smart; really, just a pleasure to be around. But as soon as Charlie got praised for this, he became the opposite: angry, violent, and hard to handle.

He desired to be unwanted. Something in him (at least at the surface level) was okay with being disappointed in. He yearned for it.

On night, while working in the kitchen, as we were cleaning up after dinner, Charlie was furious. I don't know why. I'm not even sure if he knew why. But he was mad. Livid. He wouldn't talk. He was storming around and slamming things into place.

I had told him earlier that he couldn't wear open-toed shoes in the kitchen, so he took them off. I knew this was not okay, but in my head, it was better than fighting. He still had socks on and yelled that was fine. I rolled my eyes.

He was still running around the kitchen like a madman, but then something happened. Charlie turned on the radio. He didn't ask for permission, so I almost made him turn it off, but his whole demeanor changed.

He was singing, "Cuz I'm your buckaroo; I wanna be like you, and grow as tall as you are . . . " He was working hard, sliding across the wet floor in his socks--wooing as if at his own concert.

I don't know which is crazier: that this 'soon-to-be-eighteen-year-old badass about to go in the Marines' loved country music or how easily it calmed him. I guess it's the simple things in that life that really get us, meet us where we're at, and for the moment, let us forget everything else.

May·we be as fortunate as Charlie, that with a flip of a switch or a turn of a dial, the simple things would calm us.

5 THIS, TOO, SHALL PASS

Probably one of the first things you'd notice about this young man was his desire to be at Shelterwood. He was eighteen and had a different experience than anyone else in the program. To be honest, it was his second time-- but this time, it was his choice: his desire.

Many people noticed this, welcomed and encouraged him, and challenged him to continue onward. Thankfully. And thankfully, he received the challenges and encouragement well, though I'm not saying he always did the things he should.

Another thing you might notice about Sean (aside from his charm, charisma, politeness, and seemingly abrupt honesty) was humility. And thus, a permanent reminder that "this, too, shall pass."

See, Sean had experienced many things in life, and a lot of them, he wasn't proud of. One of the most beautiful pictures of humility rested on the left forearm near the crease of the elbow of this young man.

After Sean was able to admit that heroin was not the answer--but rather, the problem: he got a tattoo over the exact spot he used to shoot up. This, too, shall pass. Because even Sean knew it couldn't solve the issues or problems in his life. He knew that allowing the addiction in his life to pass, he'd be better able to find the peace and serenity we're all searching for.

Sean was on a journey that most everyone else I know (myself included, unfortunately) is unwilling to admit they're on. A journey toward and for humility. A simple plea to be forgiven for all that led up to what we're hoping will pass.

Over and over, whenever he looked down, he was reminded. Any time I'm lucky enough to remember Sean and that tattoo, I'm reminded, too.

May·we start or continue on our journeys toward and for humility until this, too, passes.

6 YOGURT TOPS & CHOCOLATE COVERED CHERRIES

Each morning, the kids and staff went over to the dining hall for breakfast. Two days a week, there was a planned hot meal. Every other day, we had 'cold breakfast.' But even when a hot meal was served, the cold breakfast items were available: hard-boiled eggs, cereal, bagels, toast, granola bars, yogurt, and fruit.

I wasn't much of a breakfast eater, but eating an adequate breakfast was something we required of the Littles, and so, the staff ate, too. It was better than arguing over something so dumb. On the days that I had yogurt, though, I knew there was one thing I must do before I left the dining hall: wash the yogurt top and give it to Gunter.

When it was nearing Christmastime, I learned another thing about Gunter. Aside from collecting the yogurt tops, chocolate covered cherries did something to him. When he saw someone with them, he got happy; and at the same time, he was saddened.

Gunter was what one might call a high school jock. He attracted a lot of girls, and he was friends with every one he wanted to call a friend. He was often sarcastic, but mostly . . . he was sympathetic.

One of Gunter's biggest inspiritations in his life was his Mom. She gave him chocolate covered cherries every Christmas season. If I remember right, they ate them together each year.

But Gunter's Mom passed away: losing a horrific battle to cancer. And suddenly, chocolate covered cherries had a special place in my heart, too (not that I could ever understand what they meant to him).

His desire to make his Mom proud is what led to this collection of these yogurt tops. With each yogurt top mailed back in, a certain amount of money was given to help further cancer research.

There wasn't a kid in the entire program that ate yogurt without giving the top to Gunter, each time seeing the twinkle of appreciation and hope in his eyes.

In his love for his Mom, Gunter showed me each morning, we must continue fighting for what we believe in, for the things we find strength and life in, and for what we believe to be the greatest legacy we know.

May·we collect the tops. May we ask others to do the same. May we hope to help further something we believe in.

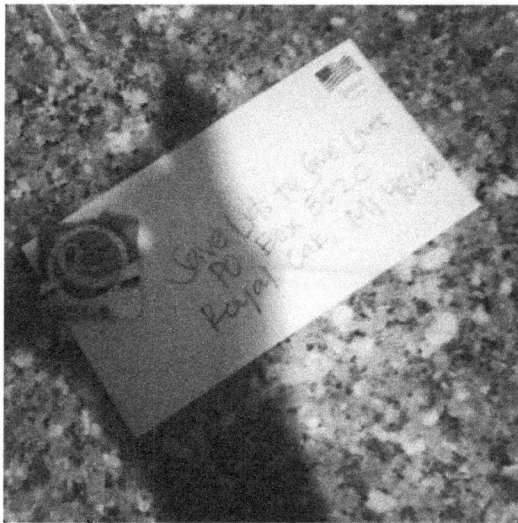

*You can still mail in the lids:

Save Lids To Save Lives
PO Box 8020
Royal Oak, MI 48068

7 PERFECTLY POISED

I had a really hard time understanding this girl: seemingly, she was perfect. I remember the day she came. I was helping her put her things away, folding clothes with her, and smiling as she told me she'd rather that shirt or those pants be folded not hung. I looked at her a little puzzled. Those clothes that she was asking me to fold were nicer than my every day attire.

She laughed and quietly told me those were her work out clothes. To me, they (at least the pants) looked as though they could be worn out and about, even fancied up. But Delilah told me that was not the case, and I continued to fold as she requested.

We joked a little while we unpacked her room. Her posture never really changed. She was the most accurately poised girl I'd ever met. Her shoulders sat perfectly aligned without a hint of knowing how to slouch. She wasn't upset with her parents for their decision to bring her to Shelterwood. She wasn't angry with God or questioning herself.

Her response was unlike any other, and it was real. She knew there were changes that needed to be made, and the home setting wasn't the place for the changes to occur.

When the other residents would speak poorly of their parents, staff, siblings, friends from home or each other, Delilah would close her eyes and inhale. Exhaling deeply, she would never partake in this negative talk--at least not in front of the Bigs. Delilah was so different. She didn't talk with her parents for months and months, and although she got frustrated, she rarely spoke ill of them.

Delilah really did dance to a different drum. And she was okay with doing so. She wore black every day. Every single day. Except, dear God, when she wore these two bright tu-tus she'd purchased at a local thrift store: one turquoise and one a melon-like orange. She loved them, and she wore them to church or to school or to the store or in her room or to the pool. In those tu-tus, I saw Delilah shine; she glowed, and she was happy.

People looked at her strangely, and her response never failed to be anything other than, "I know! I got THIS at the thrift store!" We all knew no one was trying to figure out where she got the things, but maybe why. But Delilah was so willing to come alive in that little get up. And when she smiled and desired to live life well and fully, she urged others along the same path.

You see, Delilah wasn't concerned about how she dressed, how perfect her stature was, or even what other people thought. Delilah felt comfortable and beautiful and right in her tu-tus, and when Delilah felt good, so did you.

Delilah knew the opinions of others were nothing more than opinions, and she valued them as such.

May we have the audacity to do the same. May we come alive in our tu-tus and be proud enough to share with others where they came from.

8 HIDE AND SEEK

I don't like animals. I really don't. People ask, "But you at least like (insert one animal type here), don't you?" And I have to remind them that a cat/dog/bird/horse/ladybug/butterfly/chipmunk/etc. is still an animal, and I do not like animals.

Regardless of my lack of animal enjoyment, I find beauty in some of their characteristics and can appreciate that people (myself included) and animals share some similarities with one another. There's no greater example than this: Lexi and a hermit crab.

Hermit crabs are peculiar animals. They live in a shell. But they can move to other shells: bigger shells, more colorful shells. They (as pets), most often, live in a cage. They like little rocks or things to hide under. I don't know if they like being held or not, but people do hold them. And if I remember right, they also pinch. For the life of me, I don't know why anyone would want a hermit crab as a pet.

Lexi was like a hermit crab. She was very peculiar: fun-loving and easy going, but introverted to the max, although she did not do poorly in crowds, contrary to her own belief. She used her bunk bed as her shell, and she would change the way it looked on occasion: messy, clean, more pictures, less pictures, a new letter, or a different blanket, pillow, or stuffed animal.

And every single time that Lexi wasn't around, we knew she was in her bed, hiding in her shell. But more importantly, she was waiting to be found. She knew that people would come looking for her in her shell, and she was ready to pinch be it the wrong person or topic of conversation.

But Lexi had this innate desire (although she put off the vibe of an introvert) to be with people, to be sought out when she headed for her shell or cage, and to be reminded, once again, that she was worth having. Regardless of our desires to be alone, we were created for community, and it seemed as though Lexi knew that better than any of us.

May·we surround ourselves with others who will call us out of our shells. Into more colorful places. May we go, though, to our shells if necessary. But may we always, always come out.

9 BEATS SO BIG

Communicating resident to resident (in mixed company) wasn't really allowed unless it was supervised. This obviously meant that notes were not to pass from one resident to another. And there was rarely an exception made to this rule.

Unfortunately, so much of what some of the residents had experienced before entering their time at Shelterwood had led them to some pretty unhealthy boundaries, expectations, and even allowances when it came to the opposite sex. In order to help reform these expectations and accepted behaviors, little to no unsupervised conversations were to ensue.

Except that there wasn't really a way to keep them from it. Teenagers. They know ways around things.
Humans. We're sneaky.

All that to say, notes were written, exchanged, and even responded to. Often. I'm sure far more often than the staff knew about. And the consequence wasn't steep enough to keep it from happening again and again. And so it did. It happened.

Again and again.

But I remember one note-writer in particular. He would write notes (never rude, demeaning, or 'bad,' really) to the girl he liked. He'd tell her she was beautiful and that he loved being able to see her in class or at the gazebo. He'd tell her she was worth more than she knew or believed. And then, there it was.

A line so irrelevant that had I received the letter, nothing else wouldn't have mattered. It was typically a song lyric. Something I'm sure he thought had such great meaning, depth, and breadth. Something so unfathomable that it would negate the entire nicety of the aforementioned.

Beats so big I'm steppin on leprechauns.

Because for Vinny, words gave life. And in the inability to explain them, there was mystery. And in the mystery, Vinny was engulfed, yearning, and left to desire more. Every single letter he wrote (that was found) would have some kind of line like that one. And every single time, I was reminded that in mystery, we are left intrigued. We are left searching.

We are left to figure out, to find, to endure, to ask, to wander, to wonder, to explore, to give or find meaning. We all desire meaningful lives and friends and words, right?

May·we, in the mystery, continue searching May we find the breadth that does exist. May we find it in the simplicity. And may we like Vinny, share with those who are beautiful to us that they are beautiful to us.

10 "UNCARING" AND SO CARING

Shane would be the first to tell you he didn't care. He would shrug his shoulders and tell you to go to hell or that you didn't know anything about him if you'd spend any more than thirteen seconds trying to convince him that he was caring.

Shane was funny. He was lazy. He was challenging (on purpose). He cared. He spent so much time trying to convince others that he didn't care. Shane was working hard to stay exactly where he was. No advancing through the program, and he knew that's what would happen, but he complained any way. He would complain that no one cared. And then remind you that he didn't care.

Shane did feel uncared for, unfortunately. But he was lovely. A different kind of lovely, for sure, but so lovely. Witty and jocularly, he had a comeback for every comment. He didn't always share them, but when he did, it was a treat. Except when he was doing so just to be defiant.

Shane was lovely and caring . . . and working hard to make others believe anything but these things.

I'd asked Shane about his family once. We had some similarities, and I shared a little bit about my family with him. He shrugged and nodded, which was enough to keep me talking. He continued to shrug and nod and sigh heavily. Every now and then, he'd roll his eyes. Because Shane didn't really care if our family lives were similar.

A couple of weeks later, I was having a bad day. There wasn't anything particularly wrong, but I just wasn't feeling the day. You know what that's like, right? I just felt down, bummed, and like I'd rather be sleeping than dealing with anyone at all.

Shane approached me and smirked. I faked a smile back. Oh, how I despise faking a smile. Shane commented on this smile and told me he knew how it felt. He began to replay the conversation we'd had just a few weeks earlier: reminding me of all the love and support I had from my family. He reminded me that we had similar family lives and that if he could get through the day with a real smile, I could, too.

Shane apologized for pretending not to listen and thanked me for caring. He made comments that seemed wise beyond his years about how things don't actually go in one ear and out the other. "They go in one ear and settle in my mind," he told me, "I don't let them out the other ear; I just don't always want people to think I want to know. Because knowing means caring, and caring is hard work."

He began to tell me how deeply his parents and siblings cared for him. How deeply he knew the staff cared. How much he cared. But he's right. Caring is hard work. It's a game of keeping up.

May·we care. May we invest. May we choose the hard when the easy seems better. May we let things go in one ear and settle in our minds as we care and care well!

11 PARADING THE PARKING LOT

One morning, we were having a meeting in the downstairs living room. We were talking about how things were going, things that needed to change, concerns we had, and trying to encourage one another to continue onward. And then she walked through. She was beautiful, unhappy, clothed in black, angry, and confused: Scarlett.

She spent the next several months allowing those same words to describe her. She began to open up to some of the girls and a few of the staff. She had the most incredible singing voice of any I'd ever heard. But she would rather it be muffled than heard. So, she didn't sing a whole lot, unless she didn't think anyone was listening or if it was a silly Cold Stone song I'd taught her.

It almost seemed as if she enjoyed sitting in her anger. Sadly.

She was from California. She was always cold in Missouri. But she didn't seem to mind; it was just another excuse to wear her black boots and black coat. She was fun when she let her guard down. Heck, she was fun. Period. But she didn't want to be told she was fun or pretty or nice or caring or anything complimentary.

One day, Scarlett and I went to a pizza buffet. I hated pizza buffets. Scarlett loved them. I loved Scarlett. So, we went to the pizza buffet. It was nasty out: dark, cloudy, and cold. As soon as we parked, Scarlett got out of the van, and it started snowing.

She may have never seen snow before. Ever. She began dancing. And singing. Scarlett, glowing, was dancng and singing, spinning in circles, in the parking lot. She took her coat off and began to feel the snow.

To fully *see and feel and taste* (she stuck her tongue out to catch the flakes) the snow. She longed to experience something new and cleansing. Something beautiful and unexplainable. She was tasting and seeing that which she saw as good. She was being *covered, washed, cleansed, and showered* by this snow.

I'm not trying to say the snow changed her life. It didn't. But she did, for a moment, dance and sing, twirl and spin, taste and see. *She experienced.* She lived. She glowed. She chose to fully engage. And in that moment, she was still beautiful and clothed in black from head to toe, but she was not angry or unhappy. She was living. *She was full.* She was.

And it was almost as if she knew it. Compliments, in that moment, were allowable. My hope is that we live moments like these: fully and beautifully engaged.

May·we *taste and see life as Scarlett did. May we choose to dance and sing, spin and twirl, live and engage in the moment–in the confusion. May we·stop and fully submerge ourselves in something greater and learn that we are beautiful.*

12 GOODNIGHT SHELTERWOOD

It didn't matter how late it was, how much 'trouble' he was in, or what the day before him held. Every single night, Stan would tell those he loved goodnight. He was a young boy, fourteen, if I remember right. He was funny, lively, goofy, tall, lanky, and trying to hide the fact that he was hurting.

He cared for people the best he knew how, and he hated to see anyone upset. He was open to new things and people, but he was not really willing to share much of himself. He was hurting, and he was unwilling to believe that others may have already known this about him.

Stan had come to the program even before I had. He had suffered the loss of his Mother, and although he had a great relationship with his Father and brother, he continued to suffer the loss. In this place, you come in contact with so many other people every single day. Most days, it was okay, but some days--especially the days you'd like ot hide everything about yourself, your feelings, your past, your hurts, and even your dreams--it was pure torture.

What Stan taught me, though, wasn't about hiding or smiling through it or trying to live life like something monumental hadn't happened. Instead, as he continued to do what would become his evening tradition, he taught me.

At this point, we all lived in the same house: boys upstairs and the girls downstairs. You'd think it would have been mass chaos, but it was something more rare than that: it was absolute beauty. Anyway, each night, before going to bed, Stan would go to the top of the stairway and yell, "GOOOOOOOOOOOOOOOPPPNIGHT SHELTERWOOD!"

The girls would laugh or roll their eyes, depending on their moods, and the staff responded in similar manners. Even I wouldn't come to realize how important this was to me until years later. See, every night, Stan made sure to tell those he loved and cared for good night. He made sure that everyone heard him (sometimes yelling it a few times).

The biggest lesson in it for me is this: when we care about someone or something, we say a proper goodbye, because you never know if or when you'll see it or him or her or them again. And probably, it could be argued that you may never want to do so, but if people, events, things, or places are important to us, we offer a proper goodbye.

Stan did this every night. I'm finally able to do so.

May·we, like a bold fourteen year old did, tell those we love goodbye and goodnight. May we show our love and care are more important and beautiful than pride or negligence not having us do so.

13 TWO GIRLS WITH HAMMERS, A FEW BOARDS AND NAILS

She'd been doing pretty well in the program. She had been doing her chores and talking calmly with her parents on the phone. She'd been choosing to have good, hard conversations. But it seemed as though she felt neglected, alone, and unseen.

I asked Claire if she wanted to do something, just the two of us. She did. In my head, I thought getting coffee or something was what I was suggesting. Turns out, it wasn't.

As we began to talk about what she might like to do, we headed out for a drive. She loved music. So, being in the car with just the radio was a good start. Still, I thought we'd get coffee. We didn't.

We just continued driving until we got to a hardware store. We parked and walked in. We purchased plywood. We had no idea what we were doing, but we had decided to build a shelf. Just the two of us. The gentleman cut It.

We got back to property and borrowed two hammers and some nails. We didn't even buy nails. It was so last minute. So unplanned. Claire had never built a shelf. I had never built a shelf. We were about to embark on adventure together. We went out back and began to place one board on top of or next to another. One of us holding the two boards in place. One of us hammering.

We didn't use a level. We didn't have a level. We didn't need a level. We didn't use the 'right' nails. We didn't need to. We were just going with the flow. We were laughing, and at the same time, we were serious about the task at hand. It was ours. No one else could claim it.

We kind of hurried through the project, though, because we were unsure of what to do next or how to stabilize it well.

We built a shelf. And we both carried it inside, waited to be praised, and took it to our room. We knew nothing could really go on the top shelf, but the bottom shelf could hold any heavy item we wanted!

And even if it wasn't super practical, it was ours. It started as an idea, a dream, and it became a reality. It was seen through. Beginning to end. We were proud, and we should have been. We'd stuck to it. We'd stuck through it.

And in the process, we learned something valuable: something simplistic. Things, even life, don't have to be hard or by the book or too difficult to understand. You can go with the flow if that's all you know to do. An end result can still be beautiful without instruction.

But the most important part of this shelf-building adventure was Claire's pride in the finished product. The way she protected what she'd created when someone tried to add a little too much weight to the top shelf. They way she loved this unfinished piece of furniture.

See, for Claire, she'd begun a good work. She had seen it through. She didn't need to paint or stain it to pretty it up, because the process had been so fruitful and made it beautiful. She didn't need anything more.

May we learn to trust the process, to leave things raw and beautiful. May we show off the work we've begun and be proud of the way it's turned out. Flaws and all.

14 DOULOS=BOND SERVANT

I cannot begin to describe the brilliant ways this young girl befriended others. She was caring. Selfless. Honest. Thankful. Mature. Helpful. Now, don't get me wrong, Blair could be all things opposite those attributes on a bad day. But more often than not, she was kind and selfless, giving and asking how else she could help. Blair was a true friend.

Most of us have a type of personality or certain traits we're attracted to, and so most of our friends share those traits. But not Blair. Blair befriended every one. Like I said, unless it was a bad day.

I learned so much about friendship from Blair during her time with me at Shelterwood. But my story about her goes beyond. When my time as a Big had come to an end, I worked at a camp for people with special needs and their siblings. It was an incredible place: a beautiful depiction of how we are to love one another. My job at this camp was to coordinate volunteers.

There was a week that we were short on volunteers. We called everyone who'd expressed interest in returning to volunteer that summer. The summer staff was allowed breaks from their busy schedules to call people they thought might come to help out. I called Blair. Blair had already graduated from Shelterwood and was living at home.

Blair came. Blair volunteered. She had a very difficult camper--one who was rude to her, always encouraging her to go away. She was larger and more aggressive than Blair. It was obvious that pushing her wheelchair was straining and discouraging. Blair persevered, leaving her tears and discouraged heart secretive until appropriate times. She continued to push the wheelchair, help with meals, swim with, and craft alongside the camper. She continued to encourage her and love her like the girl didn't want to be loved.

Blair was, essentially, what I'd hoped to be as her Big Sister. She was a Doulos (greek for bond servant). She continued to work alongside this girl, through the pain and difficulty. Through the discomfort and discouraging words and looks. Blair kept on giving.

Mother Theresa is known for saying, "Love until it hurts, and then love more." Henry David Thoreau is known for saying, "The only remedy for love is to love more." I have tattooed on my left wrist, "Love." Plain and simple, a command. Love. No questions, no stipulations, no payment. Blair is known (in my eyes) for acting out these sentiments.

At the end of the week, the camper hugged Blair and thanked her in a way she hadn't all week. Blair didn't do it for the praise. She did it because love is real.

May we continue to push and love alongside one another. May we choose to persevere and love beyond the hurt. May we, like Blair, love without regard to outcome and give all we have.

15 TO BE KNOWN IS TO BE LOVED, AND TO BE LOVED IS TO BE KNOWN

Maddox came to Shelterwood before I did. He even made a more difficult move than I had. He'd been in the Colorado program, which had now merged to the Kansas City property. Everything was new. Everything. The place. The buildings. The house. The people. His counselor. His church choices. The rules. Everything.

When I first met Maddox, I asked him to tell me three things about himself. The only rule of the game was that if he told me something I already knew, he had to start over . . . even if he was on the third fact. He was intrigued and played along. The first time, it was easy. I'd never talked with him. Simple facts. I have a sister. I like this band. This is my best friend.

I listened as he told me and prodded for more with each fact. I knew I'd ask to play this game again, and the more I knew about him, the harder it'd be. Plus, he was a super cool kid. The next few days, we'd play again. My sister's name is . . . START OVER. See, I'd already asked him in a previous game. It was an interesting way to learn about the kids. And usually, we'd do it in groups. To pass the time. To learn about our roommates. To learn about this community we were all apart of, like it or not.

The first month or so, we weren't even at the real property in Kansas City--it wasn't live-in ready. We were at a camp about an hour away. The girls and the boys saw each other every single day. Activities weren't even separate. They couldn't be due to the space we had available.

Soon, the property was ready, and we moved. The girls lived downstairs. The boys, upstairs. Things were a lot more separate. Regimented. *Segregated*. I still saw the boys . . . but interactions with them were a lot less frequent. A lot more formal.

One day, I passed Maddox during a co-ed dinner (which was rare). And he looked at me, thinking for a few minutes before speaking. Maybe he was trying figure out how to form the question. Maybe he wasn't sure if he should or *even really wanted to* ask. Finally, he blurts out, "Don't you wanna know three things about me, and if you already know, I have to start over?" I did.

I told him so. And I took a few minutes to talk with him. It was nice. And it was a reminder, *or maybe a lesson*, that to known is to be loved, and to be loved is to be known. It's a continually process to know and love others. You can't know someone and stop knowing them (or stop learning about them) and claim you love him well.

Maddox was so precious. So intrigued by all that was around him. He loved and cared. But he was timid in a quirky way. Bold in other quirky ways. He wanted to be known and loved. *Don't we all?*

May·we *continue to know and love and to be known and loved. That is what life is about. I can't thank Maddox enough for allowing me to do so and for reminding me it never ends.*

16 YOUNG AND UNAFRAID

Tristan was the youngest at the program. He was also among the smartest. He was willing to say and do things he believed in. Even later, I'd go on to use him as an example in empowering the kids at Shelterwood. (After my year as a Big, I left, but I returned for nearly three more!)

When I was a Big, initially, music couldn't be listened to for three weeks after a resident arrived. Even in the car. After three weeks, they could listen to approved stations and bands, and a little while after that, they were able to have personal CD players: walkmans. I'm serious. Twenty-first century. And we're allowing WALKMANS.

Tristan is unimpressed at best. He claims he copes best with music. He says he can understand limiting what kind of music is allowed, but walkmans? At level three? After that long? And not even in the car? Really? He argues the twenty-first century ploy and talks about how if they can't make good choices with music, what can they make good choices about.

He asks if residents can start having iPods. If Shelterwood can have a shared library with only approved songs. Songs picked out or approved by staff only. Or even on certain record labels. All the kids kind of laugh at his attempt to change the rules. No one changes rules, unless they're becoming more strict. No one. Rules are rules. And the staff is conservative, and they don't understand us.

Tristan writes a paper and tells the staff capable of making decisions all the reasons a shared music library and iPods can work. And he also comes up with ways to alleviate the problems. He's a real genius. And pretty soon, the music rules changed. People can listen to music in the car. And at any level. And after a while, they can have an iPod.

Certain iPods, those without internet capabilities and AM/FM radios. But they can now have iPods. They have their music back. Coping is now possible again. In a familiar way. Life, if even only for a moment, feels more normal for them.

Tristan stepped out. Spoke up for what he believed in. Spoke against what he thought was bogus. He researched and suggested. He answered questions and backed up what he stood for. He changed a rule.

The youngest. Among the smartest.

May·we choose to stand up for what we believe in, even when others stand against it. May we be cautious, honest, knowledgeable, and bold. May we choose to change things that will help us (and others) in the long run.

17 POCKETS FULL OF SUNSHINE & LETTERS FULL OF LOVE

Colt was funny: tall, semi-deep-voiced, and a little unsure. He was more like a big teddy bear than anyone I'd ever met, and at the same time, that's not a phrase many would use to describe him. He had a lot to work on and he was willing to admit it, although, he probably couldn't name those things, initially.

He would come up with almost any similarity he could find with another person just to have some common ground: some camaraderie. He'd see that you wore Adidas tennis shoes; he used to own the same pair. He'd hear you tapping your fingers against the table at dinner; he played the drums. Anything to bring him closer to another.

Colt was wooed by encouragement. He liked Sally, because Sally was nothing but encouraging to him, and she never had anything negative to say. He tried harder in school than he had previously, because the teachers worked with him, even when he didn't do so well. He would fight with his parents, but he loved his sister (no matter what), because she urged him to keep fighting.

He received mail pretty often, it seemed. He would walk around with it out in the open. I never knew who it came from, and I didn't need to know. What I did know, though, was that whatever rested inside that envelope was just as encouraging inside as it was outside: it had to be, or Colt wouldn't carry it around.

For nearly a month, Colt carried around this brightly colored piece of mail. The outside of the envelope exclaimed, "I've got a pocket, got a pocket full of sunshine." It was a popular chorus around the time. Whoa----oa---oa, the singer would go on to sing. She'd continue, "I've got a love, and I know that it's all mine. Do what you want, but you're never gonna break me. Sticks and stones are never gonna shake me."

And Colt believed this, because it was written to him, for him, about him, and over him. Encouragement does something to us. It brings us to life when other things hold us back. It shows us we're worth it when we don't feel the truth in it. Someone speaking kindly over us proves we're worth the time and effort, thoughts and breaths.

May·we choose to find rest and truth in the good things people say about us. May we do the same for others. May we walk around with pockets full of sunshine regardless of the condition of the day, and may we carry those words around proudly for as long as we need.

18 COOL, CALM, & COLLECTED: A MANTRA

I can't imagine being removed from my home as a teenager and taken to a "group home" full of people "just like me." Even the thought of it as a sixteen or seventeen year old would have crushed me. I would have been livid. I would have begged and pleaded, cried and screamed, kicked and punched. I would have been a living nightmare.

Knowing what is offered in this kind of setting though, I am so grateful it exists for the families that do need to make this difficult call. This, I'm sure, was one of the more difficult decisions for this family to make. Mark was fantastic. He was friendly with a quiet spirit and vibrant personality, kind, loving, optimistic, and fun. He really was cool, calm, and collected.

Often, you'd see Mark with a guitar. He had a better grasp of balance than I did five or six years his senior. He knew that emotion and feeling played a vital part in life. He knew, too, that there was a healthy way to express those feelings and emotions. And so, there he sat: upset, angry, happy, sad, confused . . . guitar in hand and a song in his heart, just waiting to become a healthy outlet.

Of course, the better part of this cool, calm collection Mark had was that he knew when he needed to share the songs he wrote, and when they were just for him. I am so thankful that I got to hear him sing, but even just passing him in this state without hearing anything he was singing or playing was okay, too.

Because this was Mark's thing. This is what he needed to add balance. To be in control. To know himself in the darkness we all try to hide. To be honest and bold. To be in the midst, in the depths of his deep need for better.

Mark didn't teach me to play the guitar. I wish he had! He didn't teach me how to sing. He didn't teach me how to formulate my words in such a way that others would remember them along with a jazzy tune.

What he did teach me, over and over again, though, was that life is about balance. It's about having an outlet. It's about being true to that thing, whatever it may be (journaling, singing, playing, yoga, running, drawing, etc.), and choosing that instead of ignoring the fact that something in you needs to be dealt with.

Mark showed me that being true to something you love soon overflows to other aspects and people in your life.

May we pick up the guitar and play. May we choose to find light in the darkest of days. May we sing from our hearts and cry boldly for the change we desperately need. May we find a cool, calm collection in the melodies of our journeys.

19 CLASS CLOWN: RESIDENTIAL EDITION

We've all known class clowns: the guys who do anything to get a little laughter or cause a disruption. I remember as a teenager, I had a lot of friends and could make them laugh. In college, I was even cooler. The older I get, the more it fades away, but even in my glory days, I was never as funny as Ricky.

And it wasn't even as if Ricky was the funniest person in the houses; he just really knew how to read a crowd. More than that, he gave some of the shyest people the attention no one else did. Ricky made sure every one was noticed (but if any laughter or jokes would follow, they would be at his expense). This is a skill that few possess: to give attention to anyone, everyone, the shy kids, the outcasts, the quiet guy in the corner with a sketchpad, but if anything went poorly, the joke was on Ricky.

It was almost as if he was crying out for others to be noticed, because he saw their value and their inability or lack of desire to seek the attention themselves. In doing this, Ricky took a risk. He chose to be a voice for others. He chose to exhibit the good in people that may have been overlooked.

It seems silly, but he could see six girls posing for a picture, find the one girl who looked a little uncomfortable or out of place, and jump in front of her, sorority girl pose, with a goofy grin, and make the discomfort lessen a little.

Ricky was caring. He took on the burden (and it can be a huge burden) of being the funny guy, so the other kids could be noticed for their good qualities. His quirkiness brought out a lot of silliness in others. He urged people toward a creativity that may have gone untapped (or trapped in some cases). Ricky made sure to call that which was good, good.

His anecdotes almost always portrayed a hero other than himself; and it takes a lot to humble ourselves enough to tell a story of someone else's greatness. That's what I admired about Ricky. I think that's what everyone admired about Ricky. Some class clown figures become annoying with their needs to be laughed at, looked at, smiled upon, and asked to come back for more.

But not Ricky. Of course, he welcomed feedback, laughter, jovial conservation, but I believe his true goal (intentional or not) was to bring people together in creating a safe place to be oneself fully.

May·we notice, in others, their greatness. May we live alongside one another, able to be silly, for the sake of another's strength being noticed. May we find a delicate balance, like Ricky, to not seek attention for ourselves but to showcase another when he is unable to do so himself.

20 BOLDLY BREAKING BREAD

During the summer months, the schedule was different than the school year. The residents still had summer school, but in an attempt to keep them entertained, active, happy, and healthy, each night was attributed to a certain theme: game night, house night, sports night, Bible study, etc.

For our Bible study nights, each of the Bigs had to plan two for the summer: a lesson of sorts with some kind of breadth to it. One of the Bigs was from Jerusalem (let's talk about being out of her league; I was in another ballgame!).

On this particular night, one of the Bigs had a plan to break bread with the girls: to right wrongs, to speak of and ask for forgiveness. As she read scripture to support this activity, I began to get nervous. We lived with a house full of teenage girls, who could be selfish, catty, and downright mean, if I'm honest. I didn't think this would go over well at all. I knew it was a really great idea, but I feared the hesitancy I was sure would come.

The Big explained that all you had to do was break a piece of bread from this common loaf, speak specifically about the wrong you'd done, and ask that person or those people for forgiveness. If they were willing and able to forgive you, she or they would partake in eating this bread with you. We bear others' burdens, right? And so, we break bread and share.

She sat down. I knew the awkward silence was about to start. The room was dimly lit, intimate, and full of girls who were full of wrongs (myself included). The awkward silence never came.

A young girl stood cheerfully, walked to the bread, and began her journey toward reconciliation. She told another girl she'd lied to her and had been mean on purpose. She said she knew it was wrong and couldn't really come up with a good reason to have done so. She anxiously broke a piece of bread from this previously whole loaf, and invited the girl to forgive her: to partake in this bread with her.

And the girl did.

Layla didn't hesitate to admit her wrongdoing. She was uncomfortable. You could tell it was difficult. It was also obvious that she knew it was worth it. Layla would go on her entire time having to continue in this process (without the bread), but she learned a valuable lesson about forgiveness that night, as she asked for it, accepted it, and got to offer it to another.

May·we break bread with others. May we be bold enough to break bread when we're alone. May we share in the burdens. May we ask for, accept, and grant forgiveness: for without it we are lost.

21 HOLD YOUR OWN, KNOW YOUR NAME, & GO YOUR OWN WAY

He hadn't been in the program long at all when we went to do some service projects around the community. He was with a group at a church. That church happened to be pretty close to his hometown. At some point, he ran. He headed home.

Lloyd didn't have a relationship with his parents at that point, not one involving much communication anyway, but he was headed home. He probably had more of an idea to get to one of his friend's houses, but either way, Lloyd left the building.

He was found and brought back. He did everything he was asked to do. He talked with his counselor. He did school work, chores, personal upkeep, and participated in house activities. However, he didn't talk with his folks. I wondered for a long time, if he was unwilling to talk with them, why did he run? I finally figured out in conversation with Lloyd that regardless of the relationship strain they'd experienced, he knew where he belonged and with whom.

Several months went by, and Lloyd continued to grow personally, but he was still unwilling to talk with his parents. He was unable to attain the next level without talking with them, without making an effort to better the family dynamics. He agreed to go golfing with his dad. It would be a weekend visit. I asked him if he was excited. He said no. I asked why he finally agreed to seeing or talking to them.

Lloyd knew where and to whom he belonged. He couldn't continue to progress without them, without their help. He couldn't get any closer to home, which is where he belonged, without doing the difficult conversations and face time.

He agreed because he wanted to be with them. In their home. In his home. Even when things were difficult, he belonged with them in their home. When he returned from the visit, I asked how it went.

"It was worth it." I continued to ask more questions. I wanted to know if it was fun, easy, difficult, or mind blowing. "It was worth it," he said again, "I'm the closest I've been to home in a really long time."

There's a song (Details in The Fabric) we sang nearly every week. The chorus sings, "Hold your own, Know your name, and go your own way." Lloyd did hold his own. He knew his name (and to whom and where he belonged). He just needed to go his own way.

May·we Know where we belong. May we choose to fight when it's hard, because going through the difficult battles are worth it to get the closest to home we've been in a really long time. May we hold our own. May we know our names. May we go our own ways.

22 WHO HE HAS BECOME

It's pretty easy to live in the past. But living in the past doesn't allow one to grow, to flourish, or become more. It usually takes a while for us to learn this. A lot of times, we want to move forward and hope the people who have befriended and loved us as we were will grow to love us as we are.

This rarely happens. Our parents, of course, love us as we change, but our friends are usually attracted to the things we do, portray, laugh about, participate in, and enjoy. When these things begin to change and become different than our old habits, old friends are usually the first to go. Partly because you have less in common. Partly because to grow, you must surround yourself with those who will encourage you onward.

It's hard for someone you used to party with to encourage you to stop partying while he's at a party.

The Avett Brothers sing a song, "I wanna have friends that I can trust, who love me for the man I've become, not the man I was." Theo longed for this wholeheartedly. He sought friendships that would aide him along his journey to betterment. He fought for people to see who he was becoming and love him for it. He chose to weed out friends who might try to drag him down, even when it was hard.

Theo fought for himself, because that's what becoming better is all about. When he received positive reinforcement from others, he knew they were safe to know about his journey: his struggles and his triumphs. Theo worked diligently to share his continued growth with the community he trusted.

He knew that becoming better wouldn't easily be attained by being alone. He knew he needed others to walk alongside him, to pursue hard issues with him, and cheer for him as continued to get closer and closer to his finish line. Becoming better doesn't have finish line, but it is like a race marked by miles or hardships, pain and strife, overcoming and believing. The finish line cannot be reached, but the race keeps going.

Theo believed in the changes he was making. He needed others to believe with, beside, and for him, because sometimes, believing in the changes we make is that hardest part of making the change. To this day, Theo fights for the friends who will join him on his journey, who in a sense, will make him better.

May·we search for friends we can trust that love us for men we've become. May we fight diligently for ourselves on our journeys toward betterment. May we go on that journey. May we run the race and believe in the changes we make.

23 SHOW THEM HOW TO STICK YOU

For a while, I got to be a "Med Lady." This was a glorified term for the Big who prepared and passed out medication four times a day. I loved it. There was a long, drawn out process of giving and taking medication, and rightfully so, but I did enjoy it. I really liked Tuesdays.

On Tuesdays, Kate had to get her allergy shots. One in each arm. I had never given anyone a shot. Ever. I felt a little nervous. My only instruction was coming from Kate. I would be terrified to tell an inexperienced person how to stick me. Kate was the opposite. She was in control. Maybe only with words, since my hands were doing the work, but she was guiding me.

Each time, I'd ask how I did. She was gracious. She'd say, "It was fine, but next time just a little quicker and point it like this," motioning in the correct direction. She'd show me how to hold her arm to add comfort. She was teaching me how to care well for her. It seemed ironic. I should know how to care for her. In this area, I didn't.

Each week, I looked forward to giving Kate her shots. And each time, she was patient and willing to instruct me again. She never flinched or shouted. She was calm and kind. I struggled with asking her questions, because I didn't want her to think I felt inferior. I didn't. I just got a little nervous. But each time I asked a question, she would and answer, relieved to know I cared to do it correctly.

The truth is we do teach people how to care for us. I don't think I believed or knew this until I began giving shots to Kate. She was the first person to instruct me on how to change my methods. She showed me what was acceptable. She allowed me to be hesitant. She was patient when I got nervous.

Kate wanted to be cared for in a way that most of us don't realize we need until we've experienced the opposite. She demanded respect, consideration, and a willingness to care well. She welcomed questions, because her answers led to better care. She was patient, because her patience would lead to continued care. Kate cared well for herself, and to continue doing so, she had to ensure others did the same.

May·we care well for ourselves. May we show others how to treat and care for us. May we be bold and patient. May we answer questions without judgement. And may we care for others the way Kate taught me.

AND THEN THERE WERE STILL THINGS I NEEDED TO LEARN

After my year commitment as a Big Sister came to a close, I left to work at Camp Barnabas. That place holds a very special place in my heart, and I loved the work I was able to do there, the people I got to interact with and care for. Those I had the pleasure to care with. Even so, when the summer drew near, I knew I wanted to be back at Shelterwood. I had so much more to learn, so much more to give.

After a year of being gone, a lot had changed, but I stepped into a role as House Director which would eventually lead to the Case Coordinator position, which allowed me to work with both the male and female residents. These three years continued to teach me, just as the first year had.

I had grown up a lot. I dressed more professionally; I wore my hair down. But I was still the same; however, this time, I knew I would not be the teacher. I just knew it.

Each little I met taught me a lesson, and I wish I could recount them all, but I am unable. Thank you to each resident who crossed paths with me. Thank you for your smiles, sharing your hurts, for taking your meds, for being vulnerable, and for working hard to attain a healthy lifestyle beside your family.

Thank you to the counselors for your guidance. Thank you to the families (of the residents) working diligently at home to bring your child back to you. Thank you for allowing me to know you and yours in a real way. I can never fully relay my gratitude.

24 IF ONLY MY MOM HAD SAID IT TO ME

Jill was absolutely beautiful. She looked like a barbie doll. She was fun and vibrant. She had a laugh that carried and a desire to make others happy. At the same time, she was timid. She was afraid to try new things in front of others. She had a fear that in trying something new, someone, anyone, would find fault in her.

She wanted the approval of everyone.

Jill came from a home where two others lived: her Mom and her very young brother. She loved them both very much. She spoke well of them, and it was obvious she missed them terribly. Unfortunately, she had reached a rough spot that her Mom felt unable to pull her out of, unable to help, unable to care in the best way. With that, Jill's Mom had to make what she would call the hardest decision of her life and bring Jill to Shelterwood.

Jill acted out in ways she felt confident: she was flirty with both boys and rules. She did what she was asked to do; she just never really gave it her all. She wasn't super defiant or rude; she just did the minimum. Her concern was more on what she could get away with than how well she followed the rules.

There were a few days that Jill (and some other girls) used an iPod with wifi to text people back home. Thankfully, sketchy behavior normally happened in key locations, and we were able to find out about it pretty quickly. In talking with Jill about the incident, which she denied for a long time, until I specifically spoke of an area code and a name, she admitted she was ashamed. But her shame stemmed more from how her Mom would feel.

I continued to talk with Jill. I told her that'd I'd already spoken with her Mom, and of course, she was upset, but she loved Jill. She was proud of Jill for the work she was doing. She knew going in to it, this would be hard. Jill would make mistakes and poor decisions. But she was so proud of her. I shared this with Jill, and her beautiful eyes began to fill with tears.

I asked what she was feeling. "Did she really say she was proud of me?" Yes. "If only my Mom had said it to me . . . It's all about my baby brother now, and it has to be, because he's still so young, but if she'd only said it to me . . . " and tears streamed down her face.

Really, the only approval Jill was seeking was from the one who gave it to her naturally. The one who easily, and without question, favored her. But Jill needed to hear it. We made a call together that night, and Jill heard her Mom say she was proud of her daughter.

Her demeanor changed. Her heart changed. She still acted out a little, but she had received the affirmation she'd hoped for all along.

May·we ask for what we need from those it comes from naturally, because sometimes, in the natural occurrence of their care, they may neglect to use the words we long to hear.

25 LOVE STANDS OUT

The year that I was gone from Shelterwood I got a tattoo on my wrist. Love. It's simple. The "o" is in the shape of heart. I got the tattoo in black. Often, people mistook it for permanent marker just drawn on. But it was real. A command: love.

When I got back to Shelterwood, as a House Director, I didn't interact with the boys a whole lot. A word here and there or on holidays when the houses combined to have a dinner, but it was very rare. There was a kid, Brant, who made sure to speak to me every time we saw each other. He was a rough kid. He wanted to cause problems, and he did. He wanted to be tough, and so, he tried.

One day, he asked if I had used a sharpie to write love on my arm or if it was a tattoo. I told him it was a tattoo. He grabbed my wrist and turned it to see it better. He wondered why there was a dot at the end. I explained it was a period, because I believe, if nothing else, we are to love one another. He nodded like he had some brilliant epiphany. He smiled. He kept nodding, still holding my wrist.

I pulled away gently and told him to have a good day. I turned and began to walk away. I had probably only made it five or seven steps.

"You should color the heart red."

I turned back around and asked why. He was still standing there, nodding, "Because love stands out." I let it sink in, and pretty soon, I found myself nodding, too, like I'd just had some brilliant epiphany. I began to see a different Brant that day. He hoped for and longed for love to stand out, to prevail.

The heart is now red. It will always be. It will always stand out. Rob Bell wrote this in his book, "Love Wins," and so, I hope it for Brant, and for you, and for me.

May you experience this vast, expansive, infinite, indestructible love that has been yours all along. May you discover that this love is as wide as the sky and as small as the cracks in your heart no one knows about. And may you know, deep in your bones, that love wins.

May we color our hearts red. And may we be the first to take action toward a love that stands out.

26 I GOT YOU SOME SOCKS

She was artsy and fun. She had a quirky spirit and a desire for enjoyable, yet semi-deep conversation. Esther was typically in control of herself. She was on a mission to become more comfortable in social settings and return home. She was initially free of drama.

Then something changed. I'm not sure what it was exactly. She didn't get a new haircut or do something drastic to her wardrobe. She didn't start faking her way into friendships. They just started coming her way . . . all at once. She got a different roommate. They both were artsy. Commonalities can bring people together. And maybe that's what happened. And then, she was dating a boy. And had even more friends.

She was a busy little bee and had become popular overnight, it seemed.

She still had the tendencies of an introvert, though. Sometimes, the two worlds would collide: an introvert with all these demanding relationships isn't usually an easy combination, and this is when Esther lost control. She was no longer able to control her emotion like she had. She was confused and sad. But she wore a happy smile. But her words and actions didn't back that smile up the way they had in the past.

Eventually, Esther was taken to the hospital for further evaluation. She was admitted and would stay for a few days. It was really hard to leave her there. She both wanted help and didn't. It was difficult for her to say she couldn't control herself. It was hard for her to admit the time away might help.

I visited Esther the next day to take her some clothes and to see how she was doing. She had a real smile. She seemed quiet, but her eyes were bright. I asked how she was. She said she was well. She kept looking at her feet. I asked what she was thinking. "It's so sterile here. White. Clean. Straight-edged. But they gave me these socks! And they are not like anything else in here. They kind of lift me up." She pulled her feet toward her to show the fun turquoise color and non-stick glides on the bottom. We visited for a while, but I soon had to go.

At the hospital, she was able to call anyone she wanted . . . she called the house. I answered. "It's me, Esther! I just wanted to see what you guys were doing. I'm doing really great. I get to come back tomorrow or the next day. I miss you guys." And that was it, really. The next day, one of the Bigs went to pick her up, and when she got back, she found me. She had a huge grin on her face.

"I got you some socks!"

May·we find joy in the colors when sterile, white, clean, and straight-edged stare us in the face. May we share the socks, because they kind of lift us up.

In college, I majored in philosophy. I don't remember
much: poor Dr. Furman did everything he could to teach
me well, but I wasn't the best student. I did remember
learning about tabula rasas: blank slates. It's a
concept that dates all the way back to Aristotle. Blank
slate. I got it. But I didn't get it.

Joanna was a young girl who felt alone and overlooked.
She was sassy and honest. She was funny and sarcastic.
She lived behind walls to avoid being hurt. She was
guarded. Afraid. Unwilling to be hurt again. She had a lot
to work through to get past these obstacles she'd set up
for herself. And so, she began.

One day, Joanna asked me to print a picture for her in
color. This isn't something we normally did, but for some
reason, it seemed necessary. I didn't ask questions.
Joanna liked and trusted me, but if she felt judged or
questioned her tendency was to shut down. I printed the
picture and handed it to her.

A little later, literally, a little later, Joanna came back to
me. She had the color picture, but it wasn't the same one
I'd printed for her. Instead, it was a much larger painting
of the exact picture I'd printed just a short time before.
She had started with a white canvas. A blank slate. She
created something beautiful. And as we talked about this
painting, Joanna began to let her guard down; the walls
started to shatter, slowly. But they were. Shattering.

Joanna found something that made her feel. She
loved to paint. She loved to take nothing and turn it in to
something. She enjoyed feeling the life of the very thing
she was creating. She was starting over every time.
Something new. From scratch. From nothing, she created.

She breathed life in to this thing and made it beautiful.

Tabula Rasa may be a concept that dates back all the way to Aristotle. A concept we learn about in philosophy courses. A concept that should be easily understood.

But I learned about blank slates through the life and art of Joanna. I learned about starting over, starting fresh, and breathing life into the things we care about and find beauty in from a young girl who used to live behind walls made of stone and sarcasm sharp enough to cut through nearly anything.

As I learned about this blank slate, this tabula rasa, so did Joanna.

May we start over when necessary. May we take advantage of the clean canvas. May we create something beautiful. Something worth it. Something we're proud to own. Something beautiful from nothing at all.

28 A COYOTE IS COMING! A COYOTE IS COMING!

Sheena was a young girl, who was hard to figure out. She was semi-timid and quiet. And she also wasn't. She was loud and demanding. She tried to fit in with all of the girls, and that's what confused her. Some of the girls didn't want to be around a loud, demanding youngster, and so, she became quiet and timid. Some girls didn't like that. She became what she believed was desired.

One on one, Sheena was great. She'd become honest for the first time since her last adventure, just a staff member and her. She opened up, asked questions, and listened to the responses. I enjoyed my time with Sheena, especially to doctor visits. The only thing is that if she felt she had a successful visit with the doctor, she wanted a treat. And she never had money for a treat. And because it was successful, I always gave in.

But one night, in the chaos of living in a house full of girls she felt unable to impress, Sheena did something so strange. She had just gotten out of the shower, and she came out in just her towel, which wasn't normal. It was later in the evening. She ran outside in just her towel. She ran around the house. She was "streaking." She was getting the attention of every person in the house. And this is what she wanted.

But Sheena wasn't really comfortable in her own skin yet, let alone running around outside the house in a towel. All of the sudden, Sheena was running back in the house screaming that there was a coyote chasing her.

There were no coyotes.

Sheena ran back into her room, put her clothes on, came to the office to ask for her medicine and consequences, and headed to her room for bed. She had taken a bold move. She wanted attention. But she had chosen to do something so outside of who she was that it led to discomfort and embarrassment. She went to bed. She didn't even get to soak in all of the praise and laughter she could have obtained.

The next day, the girls spoke of it, but Sheena was still embarrassed. Even the praise and laughter weren't good enough for her little stunt. She hushed the crowd quickly when it came up if she couldn't find it in herself to laugh about it. This is something that could have become a legacy. But she didn't want to be remembered for it.

May we learn from Sheena to speak up, step out, and do the things we'd be proud to be known for. May we go outside of our comfort zones . . . but only to a point that we don't need to hush the crowd for speaking of our boldness. May we leave a legacy worth remembering. A story worth being told.

29 I'M SO EX-SAD-ED!

Nikki was one of the most original people I've ever met.
She was bold and funny. She charged a quarter to sew
holes in sweatpants for other residents and fifty cents if
the job was bigger. She made everyone laugh. She played
guitar and wrote poetry. I one time asked her to write a
song for me. She sang, "Your shoes are . . . brown.
They're brown. They're . . . brown." And for some reason,
everyone laughed.

She did other crazy things that no one else could get away
with. She went to the isolation room on her on once, and
caution-taped the door closed. She would only allow
a few people in. All others would have consequences,
she'd say.

Nikki was comfortable with the girls and staff. She was
quirky like no one else. She was easy to get along with.
She always had a comeback. She was well-liked and
pleasant. But she didn't feel this way with her family. She
felt less accepted. Awkward. Alone. Unable to please
them.

Her family didn't feel this way, of course. But they all had
a long journey that had to be traveled and attempted
together. As Nikki and her family grew, trusted the
process, and became honest with one another, the
relationships seemed to flourish a little. Nikki became
nearly as comfortable with her parents as she had become
with me. She was nearing the end of her journey at
Shelterwood and coming close to a difficult and beautiful
journey at home.

When one of the residents is nearing graduation, at least in
the girls' house, we had a "Goodbye Group." This really is
a Kumbaya moment. A time where all of the girls got
together, sat in a circle, and shared stories and moments

about the graduate they wouldn't forget. In the end, the graduate could say something in return.

It was culminating event that housed tears and laughter in the sweetest form.

As each girl shared their favorite memories of Nikki: how she was the only person they knew who slept with her eyes half-open, how she won prom queen, how she boosted their self-esteem, how she made puppets as gifts for friends at home, whatever it may be, Nikki listened. And she accepted. She had helped some girls along the way. She had encouraged. She had loved. She had learned. But her time to go home had come.

Nikki cried, literally, cried, "I'm so ex-SAD-ed!" And it was as if it wasn't planned: this pun. But she was. She was sad and excited. So were we.

May·we move to greater things. May we experience deep change. May we be sad to leave and excited to go. May we move in a Kumbaya moment and trust that the process has gotten us where we need to be before the next adventure.

30 THANKFULNESS COMES YEARS AFTER

About a year and a half after this girl had graduated, I received a text message. It went something like this:

"Thank you for doing what was hard. Thank you for not giving up. Thank you for giving consequences we deserve. I know it probably seemed like we didn't care, but we did. Thank you for being the one to enforce hard rules. A year later, it still means a lot."

I was in a staff meeting, and the message completely caught me off guard. This was one of the most polite young people in the house during her time. She had some boy drama, sure. She wanted to be in relationship with them to help them feel good or normal or right. But one, she knew was an okay relationship to enter; and the other, not so much. The "not-so-much" relationship" is the relationship she desired to be part of more. She knew he was worth knowing.

This bad boy. But Mona knew he wasn't so bad. He was just unknown. He was lost. He was scared. He was fearful. She wanted to find him and to call him to a place without fear. She was young: seventeen. She was in no place to find lost a young man. But she wanted to save him. She wanted to be saved herself.

Mona learned a lot during her time at Shelterwood. She was very honest with her counselor, and she was very honest with her parents. As she became honest in those relationships, she was no longer able to hide that honesty from herself. Mona knew she had some things to work on an through. She knew there was some hurt and confusion that must be dealt with. And she began to do this difficult task.

Staying true to this task meant no relations with or trying to save this boy. Mona had to focus on herself. She had to be found. It was a beautiful finding. A beautiful reunion with her family. A beautiful acceptance of who she'd become.

And a year and a half later, she was thankful. She wasn't a difficult resident. She was fun and energetic. She was able to have a good time under nearly any circumstance. But she had come to know that although there may be pain the evening; joy comes in the morning. Although suffering comes first; it is followed by triumph.

May we know that thankfulness comes next. May we rest assured that there is joy in the morning. May we know that the trial is prevailed by the triumph. May we know that if a fight is not fought, no journey is won. May we rest in tomorrow's joy and be thankful to those who journeyed alongside us even if they don't accept our thanks.

31 PROUDLY DONE & WITH FOND MEMORIES

Callie was the life of the party. She knew how to have fun, and partly, that might be a reason she'd come to begin her journey at Shelterwood. She was smart, too, studious, and ambitious. She knew she work to do.

Her brother had been a resident at the program a year or two before her, so, she was aware it would be a difficult process. Thankfully, this urged her forward instead of hindering her progress.

Callie made friends easily. She was kind and loving. She also cared about her schoolwork and planned to graduate high school and the program, which she did! She took care of herself, ate pretty well, and visited the gym often. She also allowed a few of the Bigs to invest heavily in her life. She was honest and open.

She fought hard to get what she'd set out to find. She worked well with her family and her counselor. She searched within herself to address deep matters that we're all afraid to touch. Callie was a bold and daring seventeen-year-old, willing to attempt an unadulterated life change, because she believed she was worth it. Thankfully, she surrounded herself with people who reminded her of this truth when she was doubtful.

Callie finished the program two days shy of seven months. She fought hard and well. She sought answers to difficult questions: even from herself. She had to accept things she didn't want to believe at times. She had to know that life would be different when she got home. She had to ask for and hope for different.

Callie was completely respectful and thankful to the staff at Shelterwood. She was accepting and gracious.

The night before she graduated, she took a picture near the entrance of Shelterwood. She was using both hands to gracefully flip (flick or however you say it) off the Shelterwood sign: the place, the journey. She had finished it. She was done. She had given everything she could have. But her time had come to a close, and she was thankful.

She proudly displayed this picture. But only once. The cooler thing about this is that it wasn't Callie's attempt to be ornery, rude, or resentful. She was telling the journey she had won!

Since this picture, Callie has posted another picture (more than once): a telling picture, one worth thousands of words. This picture captures her holding her graduation certificate with the proudest of smiles. The caption always announces her happiness and pride of this accomplishment.

May we fight hard. May we surround ourselves with the hopeful for the times we feel nothing but doubt. May we tell the journey we won. May we humbly show off our accomplishment, and like Callie, may we look back with pride and happiness, knowing the journey is worth the difficulty.

32 THE MOST GENTLE STRONG MAN

Danny was seemingly an oxymoron. You'd see this young man with a football build carrying boulders around the loop, moving them from this place to that one, or trying to push one of the minivans. He was strong. He was known for being angry. He was supposedly aggressive. And seeing his ability to move these mountains, one might think those assessments were true.

Until you talked with Danny. He was soft spoken, quiet, kind, and shy. He would admit he struggled with anger, aggression, and disrespect. But upon meeting him, talking with him, and continuing alongside him, it was difficult to believe those qualities ever existed in this young man.

I didn't know Danny immediately. I didn't talk with him for a little while after he came. Maybe the qualities had begun to fade before I met him. As I continued to know him, though, I learned that Danny had learned to channel his anger and frustration. He learned to use his strength for good. He'd chosen to become quiet and well-tempered.

He'd become comfortable with his strength and the abilities that came with it. He no longer felt the need to be strong due to his size. Instead, he became strong in his humility. He was moving these huge rocks and cars in order to train for the Young Strong Man competition he wanted to compete in when he returned home.

He had made a conscious decision to get better, fitter, extra capable, and strong in more ways than the one way he'd previously known: the one he used to belittle others. This spilled over into other aspects of Danny's life. He began to desire calmness. He quenched for it. He demanded it in the gentlest of ways, even in relationships . . . especially in relationships.

When Danny's family came to visit, they couldn't believe who he'd become. They noticed he'd been calm with them during phone calls. But I would imagine it'd be pretty difficult to trust the change. They questioned its permanency. I would, too. It was a real change for him. It was a pleasant change for them.

I'm not sure if Danny participated in this competition when he returned home. I hope he did. I hope he did well. And if he didn't compete or didn't do well, I hope he's reminded of his training. All the conscious decisions he made to be better than he'd been.

May we give all of our strength to find our humility. May we, like Danny, be strong and may we be gentle.

33 DON'T APOLOGIZE FOR WHO YOU ARE

A young, cheerful girl lived in a young, cheerful body. Miley was full of adventure and a desire to jump, tumble, run, and play. She took gymnastic lessons a couple times a week and cheered competitively at home. She was talented, continually learning and growing that talent.

Miley was often found in the living room of the house. Although she was younger than most of the girls, she was further along in the program and had more privileges. She could be alone in her room, but typically, she didn't choose to do so. She wanted to be in the know when someone walked in. "Hey girl!" was her go-to-greeting, unless, of course, it was a boy. She acknowledged everyone . . . because she wanted to be acknowledged.

If any look was exchanged with Miley, that she didn't take as positive, she would apologize. She didn't know what she was apologizing for, but she wanted to make it right. Miley wanted to be acknowledged and liked. One thing we continued to encourage Miley to do was to know why she was saying she was sorry so much.

It even got to the point where most of the girls wouldn't respond to Miley's apology with anything other than a simple question. "What are you sorry for?" If she couldn't answer the question, she was reminded to not apologize. Sometimes, others will not be happy and may look sad or frustrated. That has nothing to do with you, we'd tell Miley.

Eventually, one day, for some reason, Miley chose to be alone. After a little while, she came out into the living room, announced her arrival exclaiming, "Hey girls," and then sat down. She looked pensive. One of the girls asked her what she was thinking about.

I'm so grateful I was in the living room.

And in a small voice, seeking approval, and so full of wisdom, Miley cleared her throat. "So, are you guys just trying to tell me not to apologize for who I am and only to apologize for the things that corrupt that?"

Jaws dropped. My eyes widened. The girls exploded with pride for Miley's depth of understanding. Finally. They clapped. Miley loved this. She couldn't stop smiling. She had finally gotten what we'd all been trying to tell her . . . but the realization was her own.

May·we listen to others when they direct us well. May we dig into those directions ourselves to truly figure out what they actually mean. May we not apologize for who we are . . . but only the things that corrupt that.

34 PIN THE TAIL ON THE DONKEY OR THE KISS ON JOE

Every Friday night, we had hall night. Hall night could be really fun. Hall night could be really boring. A lot of times, my girls just wanted to watch a movie and get free food. I could understand, but I wanted to change it up sometimes. We'd go on scavenger hunts, over to staff houses to play the Wii or paint pictures on their walls, or write encouraging messages to one another on super large panties.

Typically, my ideas were received well, after a few minutes. One day, I had a brilliant idea: a sleepover! Except we would all go to bed on time in our own rooms. But we would have raw cookie dough, candy, popcorn, and soda. We would jump on the beds and watch a chick flick. We would play board games and a teenage sleepover rendition of pin the tail on the donkey. Pin the kiss on Joe.

Joe worked in the Guys' House and just happened to be walking by before my sleepover. This was obviously a last minute idea. I told him I needed to take his picture without any explanation. He was cool with that. I printed it. I hung it on the wall in the sleepover room. I grabbed some extra paper, scissors, and super bright red lipstick. This was legit.

I waited until we were completely in sleepover mode before talking about the game. I explained, we'd all put on the lipstick, kiss the paper, cut out our lips, be blind-folded, spun around a few times, and then pin the kiss on Joe.

Whitney was appalled. She was not pinning her kiss on Joe. She was not. She would not. She didn't even want to put the lipstick on. We all convinced her it was a game. Joe didn't even know what it was, and it was innocent, silly, kind of dumb, but fun. Whitney drew lips. She drew lips onto the paper and cut them out.

Whitney was funny. She was shy. She was quiet. She was uncomfortable. We all encouraged her to do it with us, and she decided she would. And when she did it, she laughed and seemed to enjoy this silly game. We were all laughing with each other as we attempted. No one was completely successful. But laughter (when shared) is successful, and so, I guess it was.

Whitney was adamant that know one hear about her pinning the kiss. However, after the game was over, she didn't care. It didn't mean anything. It was a game. It was something we could do and laugh about together.

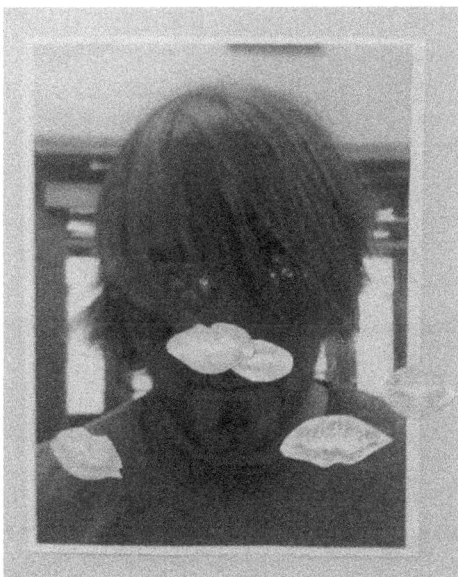

May we be cautious, like Whitney, about the things in which we partake. May we trust those we're with and laugh about the ridiculousness of silly games. May we enjoy simple twists to childhood memories and never grow too old or shy to do so.

35 WE'RE ALL IN THIS TOGETHER

She was defiant from the beginning, always talking back and trying so hard to make others believe she was the boss. She was quiet in group settings, which she probably thought would help her sneak away. She kept a quarter from her home state hidden in her pillow case. She was bound and determined to get away.

Virginia made me laugh. She pretended like she didn't want to make me laugh. But when I wasn't around, she'd ask about where I was and when I'd be back. She trusted me. She trusted Amy. Amy and I spent a great deal of time with Virginia. It was difficult and it was enjoyable.

Virginia attempted to run several times. She never really got too far . . . except the one time she did. She was found quickly, and obviously, this upset her. A part of the consequence of running away is having your belongings taken away for a while. You'd only be left with the bare essentials. Even your clothing and closed-toed shoes are taken. A jumpsuit becomes the new wardrobe. Virginia wasn't okay with this. She refused to change.

Amy and I sat in the living room with Virginia pacing around us, quarter in hand. She was surely showing us she was in charge. She paced and paced. She found soda on the table and poured it over our heads. She laughed, but it upset her when we didn't get angry. She wouldn't sleep. She wouldn't eat. She wouldn't do anything unless it was her idea. Finally, she was ready to shower.

Virginia went to shower and left her clothes in the toilet stall. I changed them out for a jumpsuit. Amy and I waited for her to finish. A few minutes later she comes out of the bathroom in just her underwear. "I can't believe you would take my clothes," she says, "at four in the morning!" And she was serious. She thought she'd outsmarted us, out-waited us. She believed that she wouldn't have to wear the jumpsuit.

She sat, exasperated, in the chair. The next morning, she still refused the jumpsuit. Amy and I had a talk. We decided that if it'd motivate Virginia to wear her jumpsuit, we would wear them, too. All she had to was agree to wear it for the week. Amy and I walked in with jumpsuits on and threw one to Virginia. She smiled and dressed in the navy blue suit and headed to school with the rest of the girls. She wore the jumpsuit all week.

All she needed was to know and believe she wasn't alone. All she wanted was, although it was never verbalized, to know we were in this together.

May·we walk alongside others in jumpsuits. May we carry our state quarters and hope like hell to back to where we belong. But may we trust the process, the people with us, the jumpsuits, and all it encompasses.

36 MUD & PUZZLES=TRUE GIFTS OF LOVE

Deborah was kind and polite when I first met her. She was beautiful and unique. She was young and yearning to grow into her own person. Eventually, after a while, Deborah began to act out, show off, and purposefully get in trouble. She had found the attention she enjoyed, and she worked any angle to get it.

She'd become aggressive and unthankful. She, by all measures, seemed to have regressed. She was resentful. And she was showing her parents that if they thought she needed help, she'd make them pay. It was quite something. It was terrifying: the power she held in this bold attempt to be someone even she was unfamiliar with. Every now and then, there'd be a glimpse to the horror she felt, but she squashed it quickly and continued acting out.

Deborah's parents were wonderful, patient, and kind. They weren't proud of her actions; but they were proud of their daughter. Her Dad often traveled to Israel for work. Now, that's a cool job! For Deborah's birthday, her parents sent gifts. They were unable to be with her to celebrate. I was able to take the gifts to her room and allow her to open them with her roommates.

Deborah (at this point in her stay) was 'better' than any gift that could be given. I was so nervous for what was about to happen. She opened her first gift. It was a bath set. From the Dead Sea. Where her Dad traveled often for work. I squinted my eyes and waited to hear some dramatic outburst about this not being a good enough gift. It didn't happen. She smiled. She was thankful. She asked to call and thank her parents.

She opened the next gift. It was from her brother. It was a puzzle. I knew for sure she'd be upset. I was wrong. Deborah admitted she didn't like puzzles as much as her brother did. But she was so thankful that he'd thought to get it for her. Knowing how much he enjoyed puzzles, she felt loved. She offered to allow her roommate (who really enjoyed puzzles) to work the puzzle. She couldn't wait to use the mud bath. She was so humble. So thankful.

She kept saying she didn't deserve these gifts. I was so proud. Going to this little birthday celebration, I was in a state of dread. I was sure Deborah wouldn't appreciate any small gift. She'd grown so entitled. I was wrong. I was humbled. I was thankful. Deborah had a phone call with her parents to thank and share a small portion of her birthday with them.

These gifts called Deborah back to a place of reality. Back to a truth of who she was. Back to a place where she was appreciative and undeserving.

May we appreciate the mud and puzzles. May we know that sometimes, although the gifts aren't what we'd choose, they mean a lot to the chooser . . . which means we mean a lot to the chooser. May we learn from Deborah to accept, with gratitude, the gifts we don't deserve from those who love us regardless of what we ask for.

Cade was a young man who had made incredible progress. The first time I ever met him, he was playing an intramural game of indoor softball, and he thought I was unfair. He was loud about this stance, too, as he stormed out of the gym yelling that he was not out. (He came back to apologize.)

Months later, Cade was heading home for a visit with his family. It wasn't a break, so he was the only one at the house, waiting to leave for the airport. I sat with him for a few minutes while the Big went to the dining hall to grab the two of them lunch. He asked if I'd like to play jenga.

Sure. I hadn't played jenga in years. I don't even really know the rules. Are there rules? If it falls, you just start over, right? Anyway, I said yes. Cade and I built this tower out of blocks. Strategically placing them to stand firm. To stand tall under attack, so to speak. It got pretty tall. It stood well.

I thought it was a good game. And then Cade asks if I'm ready. He begins to take one block out of the formation we just built. Your turn. Right. My turn. I take off a top block, because I'm semi-chicken of the tumble.

Cade blows me away.

"Isn't it weird? Life is kind of like jenga. We keep building on all the things we know. And one day, we make a decision or a lot of decisions that have the ability to make it all collapse. Sometimes, we don't even make the decision. Maybe our parents did. Or maybe it was a bad grade. Or saying no when we should have said yes. I just think it's weird how we do so good for so long, and one thing can make us fall all the way back to where we started."

He's right. We have a foundation, whatever it may be, and we build on it. All of life is built on it. We make decisions and add another layer. We say yes and keep going. We say no, and our towers get taller. We go here or there, and our foundation gets shaky. We remove a friend, a habit, a quality, and we either become stronger or weaker.

I had never compared life to jenga before. I had no reason to do so. But on this day, with Cade, it was clearer than any other illusion or description. He was anxious about his visit home. He was excited, but going for a home visit was always a way to build on or tear down the tower you'd been building at Shelterwood.

May·we stand firm on our foundations. May we believe in that which we're rooted in. May we build on this foundation and choose to build it. May we make choices that, even when removing, our foundation is strengthened. And may we enjoy this game of jenga in a way we never have before.

38 HALFWAY ACROSS THE WORLD TO SAY THE SAME EXACT THING

Sloane was one of the most caring and compassionate young ladies I've ever met. She was hurting and burdened. But so much of this hurt was brought on my her own attempt to carry the weight of the world (and all of the other girls) on her shoulders. Literally. So often, I can remember being proud of Sloane for talking one girl out of self-harming only to find Sloane doing so later. She hurt for others. She hurt for herself.

Her parents loved and cared for her. They tried so hard to make her understand the depth of their love and care, but for some reason, it wouldn't resonate with Sloane. She didn't believe it. It didn't compute, and it didn't make sense.

During the year, there are two family retreats for each house. Semi-last minute, Sloane's Dad decided he would come to the retreat which was approaching. He was stationed in a foreign country for the military, and he had a job that not many could do. He also had a daughter that needed to see him. Thankfully, he made the decision to take leave, travel to the retreat, and spend time with his daughter who couldn't understand the gravity of his love for her.

Sloane was confused by how she felt about her Dad coming. Was he just coming because she'd been acting up? Did he feel obligated? Would he come to punish her for acting poorly? He came. She was astounded. He was so loving and kind. He was so compassionate and caring. He asked questions and listened to her answers. She was cared for (like she'd been all along), but it felt different.

Every Sunday, during Family Retreats, there's a share time. It's a beautiful time. Parents share. Siblings share. And most of all, the kids who have been shut down share. It is a time of healing. Accepting. Saying. Believing. It is beautiful. It can be awkward. Tears are shed in each row, and hearts are slowly mended.

On this particular Sunday during the Family Retreat, Sloane stands up. With the microphone in her hand, she says, "It's been a really good weekend. My Dad flew half-way across the world to spend time with his delinquent daughter, so, I guess he kinda likes me."

Her Dad is humbled. He is proud. He is teary-eyed and touched. He stands. He hugs his daughter, really, for the first time in probably what felt like far too long. And he says, "I don't just like you; I love you." He'd been saying this all along. They hug. People cry. I cry. Sloane accepts this love. I hadn't seen anything so beautiful in quite a while.

May·we trust what's being said by those who love us regardless of the distance they travel. May we choose to accept the love that's difficult to understand. May we find hope in the fact that others are for us, even when we act out. And may those who love us be patient as we battle against them due to our own fears and confusion.

39 SERVING TIME FOR NO REASON AT ALL

She had returned from a weekend visit with her family. Her trip was really great, she said. Her drug test came back positive. In talking with her about this, she was livid, confused, and positive there could be no way it would be true. I had to call Roxy's parents. They were saddened. They were also confused. They were sure Roxy hadn't done anything. She was with them the entire time . . . except one hour or so.

The three of them fought it. They continued to think about all the things that could have caused a false-positive. Was it this or that or even the orajel? I was sad, too. She was doing so well. She was so close to going home. But she tested positive. We sent of the urine to confirm and asked her to serve the drug consequence.

I fully expected she'd fight it. I knew her parents would, if they truly believed it was unjust. And they wanted to. But they said, "Roxy's come a long way, and we've fought a lot of battles for her. A lot of battles with her. We don't think she did it. But this one is her's. We'll be interested to see how she handles it."

Roxy continued to deny the accuracy of the drug test. She refused to say she had used any substance. She was adamant. I believed her. But she had never falsely tested positive before. Her medicine hadn't changed. It was so weird. Roxy served the time. She did room grounding, house grounding, property grounding, and work hours. She made silly remarks, of course, but she was never rude. She had (for the moment) changed her middle name to "Room Grounding."

To this day, I have no clue if Roxy actually used during that break. To this day, she says she didn't. I believed her then. I believe her now. But what I do know is that she graciously served these consequences, right or wrong, and didn't speak ill of the process. She claimed her innocence. She used the time well.

She may have been wrongfully accused. But Roxy had already grown so much. She pleaded her case. She claimed to have not used while she was at home. She still did what she had to do in order to be compliant. I was so proud. She may have served so many undeserved hours.

Regardless, she did them without complaint. I was impressed with Roxy's parents, too. I'm sure if they pressed us to not consequence her; we wouldn't have. They didn't. They said they'd fought too many battles for her. This was her thing.

I love this family. I have been extremely blessed by this family. I have been changed, challenged, fed, and loved by this family.

But in this particular thing, I learned that sometimes, people won't be able to trust us because of a simple test, although our actions speak more clearly.

May·we speak for ourselves of the things that are true. And if there's no way around it, may we, like Roxy and like Paul of the Bible, do the time without complaint, knowing that lives will be changed by our sacrifice.

40 WATCHING IT GROW

Patrick was a funny kid. He practically lived in pajama pants and flip flops. He dreaded his hair and colored it blue. He loved to cook and make people laugh. He enjoyed seeing others happy, although he probably would have a difficult time admitting it. He knew what he wanted and what he didn't. He wanted to be in control. He played cards and twisted his hair. He wanted to be under the influence (any influence) and forget everything else.

One day, I told Patrick I would give him a prize. I can't remember why I was giving him a prize. But each time he saw me that day, he asked about it. I told him to be patient; it would come. I searched around my office. I asked the house directors if they had anything. I didn't want to just give him candy or a soda. I wanted a prize. A good one.

Patrick was playing cards with several of the boys in the busy living room. I walked into the group. I handed Patrick a plastic cup with a small amount of water in it. "This is my prize?" It was. Partly. I handed him a little yellow capsule. "Is this gonna grow into something in the water?" It was. It was silly, but I thought he would like it.

He took a break from the cards. He dropped the capsule into the water. He held the cup gently in both of his hands. He watched it with his eyes wide. He kissed the cup and sweet talked the capsule, not knowing what it would become. Only that it would become.

It started to grow. A little yellow . . . antelope, maybe. He allowed it to grow a little more. He continued to watch it. He named it. He took the little guy out of the cup and held it up for everyone to see. To admire. It was his. He had watched it grow into what it was designed to become.

In a matter of minutes, he was able to see the process of growth.

As time passed on, as small a token as it was, it still meant something. Patrick would tell me it was on his desk. It was doing fine. It was a silly little prize. But giving it to Patrick and watching him watch it, seeing it grow and become, I learned that we're all like this. We all long to see something from start to finish. We want to watch the growth. We want to nourish something or someone to life. We want to be a part of the process and a part of the growth.

May·we, like Patrick, in the midst of cards or friends, take a moment to help nourish and grow things. May we do the same for ourselves and those in our lives. May we speak kindly and wait patiently. May we enjoy seeing the growth and make it known.

41 SING FOR THE MOMENT

I had the pleasure of speaking at Hadley's graduation. It was a difficult speech to give, not only because Hadley had come to mean a great deal to me, but also because she had worked so hard to go home. To become healthy. To trust herself. To trust her parents. I used some lyrics from several Eminem songs to celebrate Hadley's progress and accomplishment. I feel it's the best to do so now, as well.

Upon her arrival at Shelterwood, Hadley was so used to 'losing herself in the moment, she owned it, she never let it go.' She had learned to be the boss. She rarely asked for permission from her parents and held little to no regard for what they asked of her.

Thankfully, this didn't last too long. Eventually, Hadley became honest. She worked with the people who were for her. She moved onto the next Eminem songs, and although she didn't cry these exact words, she did these exact things.

'I got some skeletons in my closet, and I don't know if no one knows it. So, before they throw me in my coffin and close it, Imma expose it.' She began to share some things that her parents knew and some they didn't. She continued on this dreary path for a while. 'I'm sorry, Momma. I never meant to hurt you. I never meant to make you cry, but tonight, I'm cleaning out my closet.'

And Hadley cleaned well.

In parts of her cleaning, she felt alone. Through some of it, she felt over-watched. She was on a mission. And cleaning a mess that's gone unnoticed for too long is never easy to work through.

But my favorite lyric appropriate for Hadley's triumphant cleansing comes next. And it's my favorite because Eminem spits it with such conviction and because Hadley's life reflected it. And I just can't keep living this way. 'So, starting today, I'm breaking out of this cage! I'm standin up; Imma face my demons. I'm mannin up; Imma hold my ground. I've had enough, now, so fed up: tryin to put my life back together right now.'

Hadley had people to walk alongside her. People to remind her she was facing her demons. People to help her hold her ground. And she'd learned how to keep the skeletons out of the closet and who she could trust with those secrets.

When I was in high school, Eminem challenged me, when Hadley was graduating I challenged her, and today, the challenge is for us all:

'If you had one shot, one opportunity, to seize everything you ever wanted in one moment, would you capture it or just let it slip?'

May·we capture it. May we clean out our closets. May we stand up and man up and face our demons and stand our ground. May we invite people near. May we lose ourselves in the moments safe enough to lose ourselves in.

42 A DAD DELIGHTS IN HIS DAUGHTER

Mary was in her late teens when she started the program. She was able to have great scholastic success. She finished high school and started college. She was a fun girl! And her self-esteem was definitely boosted by entering college.

She was doing well, taking classes seriously, meeting friends, having time off property with a girl from her class, and learning a lot about herself. I had the privilege to know Mary pretty well. She let me in. She allowed me to know the real her. She felt comfortable with me there.

One day for counseling, she got to go out to eat. I was invited. Thai food. Of course, I said yes. I liked Mary, the counselor, Thai, and the challenges presented in counseling sessions (because I believed in them). The three of us ordered and indulged in a little small talk. Finally, once our orders had arrived, the counselor did her thing.

"How's it going, Mary? Like really?" She said it was fine. You know, school was fun; she liked hanging out with her friend. She was ready for a break to go home. Her relationship with her Mom was so wonderful. And her Dad was a good dad. But when she spoke of their relationship, it was different than when she brought up her Mom. Thankfully, the counselor is intelligent.

"Why do you get excited to talk about your Mom and quiet when it comes to your Dad?" Mary was quiet. So quiet. She didn't say anything. We both looked at her. She looked at her food. She cleared her throat slightly, "He's a good Dad." He she went on to say that they talked when he was home, but most of her conversations were with her Mom.

I think I'm smart, and so, I chime in about Captivating, which is a book I was made to read as a Big. A book that really talks about a daughter being delighted in by her father. As I spoke about this, Mary's eyes welled with tears. She longed to be delighted in by her father. She longed deeply. We suggested the three of them read the book.

I'm not sure if they did. Mary was supposed to bring it up on her next phone call. I don't know if it ever happened. I hope it did. I know Mary went home after a while with intentions of continuing school and building on the relationships she'd built with her parents.

But she left that lunch knowing she longed for something she didn't have. She left Shelterwood knowing it was something she wanted. I hoped she spoke of it: asked for it.

May·we, in our humility, ask to be delighted in. May we know we're worth being delighted in. May we trust others when they tell us so. May we delight in ourselves. May our eyes fill with tears, knowing we are worth the delight of our fathers, our friends, our loves, and ourselves.

43 IF IT LOOKS BAD ON YOU

I loved being the Case Coordinator. It was a demanding job that allowed me to work with every student. It was more than forty hours a week, and I thrived outside the regular nine to five. Tim had been at Shelterwood for a while. He trusted me. But he liked being in control.

This wasn't always an issue. But a few times that I can recall, Tim refused to take his medicine. He wouldn't go to school. He just wanted a butter-drenched bagel and to relax. He wanted to call the shots. At an attempt to not cause a fight, the Bigs did not argue. They documented he didn't take his medication. They let the appropriate staff know he'd stayed at the house instead of going to class. And they stayed with him.

As soon as I got word that Tim had pulled his little shenanigan again, I was in his room with a guy staff member and all of his medicine. "Tim," I'd say, "I know you don't want to take your medicine, and I'm not sure what's going on, but do you trust me?" He did. I would remind him that I obviously didn't prescribe any of the medication, but doctors I respected did. I would ask what the issue was.

Usually there wasn't one. He just wasn't feeling it that morning. "So, I didn't prescribe these, but you know that I scheduled the appointments, talked with the doctors, your parents, and your counselor, and everyone has agreed these are good medicines to try for now. Obviously, you can refuse, and we'll continue to spend the day as we are now, but if you trust me, and I trust the doctors, and your parents, maybe you could think about taking the medicine?" I'd continue to talk about how if he wasn't taking it, it would look bad on me--the med lady. He didn't buy it. And that's okay. I wasn't selling anything.

Finally, he'd look at me. "So, if I take it, essentially, your job is done well?" I'd answer, essentially. He would hold out his hand, wait for the pills, put them in his mouth, drink the water to wash them down, cough, and show me his mouth. And then remind me that I did a great job.

I wasn't trying to bribe Tim. I was trying to remind Tim that he was cared for by a team of people, including his prescribing doctor. He knew those things. But he liked me. He cared that people would think I did or didn't do my job well. If he could contribute, he would. But the funny thing is that after he took his medicine, he was ready to face the rest of the day: school, counseling, no bagel. It didn't matter. He'd bettered someone's reputation.

Tim didn't refuse his medicine for me. He refused it for control. He didn't take it for me. He took it to be a part of something. To be a part of a team he trusted. To allow others to trust me. And to start his day the way it should have started.

May we add to the reputation of others. May we believe that those we trust are for us. May we stick with our routines and allow others to care for us when control seems more appealing. May we do as we should and remind others that we're proud to be a part of their good job.

Summer was a beautiful young girl, reminding me of Kelly Kapowski from "Saved By The Bell." She was fun and had a dry sense of humor. She liked bands I'd never heard of and had ridden elephants. She was internally angry. She had a gorgeous smile and an inviting personality.

She did what she was asked. She excelled, because she believed in herself. She did what came naturally to her. Eventually, as her anger subsided, the familial bonds become easier and more natural. She was set. Smooth sailing. School, chores, and even family relations were good.

A family retreat was just around the corner. A trip to Haiti was soon after. She claimed to be excited for both. Smooth sailing. A new perfume had just come out. She had it and said she had for a long time. She was caught. Stopped. Amidst rough seas. Smooth sailing no longer. The retreat no longer mattered; neither did the trip to Haiti. She was found. She ran. Literally.

Summer spent an entire day running away. It was impressive, to say the least. She'd talked a couple of neighborhood kids into thinking she'd lost her phone and needed to meet up with some friends about twenty miles away.

She got to her desired location, dyed her hair in the restroom, and continued to galavant around, thinking (knowing) she wouldn't be found.

We searched. We prayed. We cried. We called her parents. They reacted like we had. We continued to search. Her parents tried to decide if they should cancel their plans to come for the retreat. They didn't. We'd called the police. We were in the woods and on the streets. We were on the phones. We questioned the girls after school. No one knew anything.

Even the girls Summer told everything to were clueless.

After the ten hour search, we had everyone come back except for two girls. They walked into a coffee shop to use the restroom, where they found Summer. They brought her home.

Summer washed the dye out of her hair and listened to the police officer. She was welcomed with big hugs and tear-filled eyes. She couldn't believe the girls were worried. I think she thought everyone was as hard as they said they were. Having twenty girls welcome her home was the best thing that could have happened.

She really couldn't understand their care for her. She was a part of this family. A part of this house and these girls' lives. And of mine. She questioned us. So, you guys were like really worried for me? Our response was unanimous.

In our worry, Summer felt loved. She didn't feel like she was overbore with eyes not trusting her. Instead, she felt what it was to be cared for. She accepted the love.

She was glad to be home.

May·we accept the love others give. May we accept that worry is usually a sign of care. May we keep others in the loop . . . at least a little. And may we be glad to be home.

45 YOU BEDAZZLE ME

Harper was a funny girl. She was continually learning about herself, and the things she hoped to stand for. She had a group of followers whether she wanted them or not. A little fan club of those she called her friends. People wanted to be like Harper, and they wanted her approval.

Probably because Harper had a keen ability to make one feel as if she was on top of the world on her most doubt-filled day. Harper was sarcastic. She was incredibly crafty with her words. Her tone was the key to the sarcasm, but when Harper gave a compliment, it was sincere. And it was unlike any other.

You bedazzle me.

She once made a pair of sweatpants for a house director. It was her gift welcoming the girl into the position of "greater importance and responsibility," although any good house director would argue such. Fancy pants, she called them. On the pants, she'd written it. You bedazzle me. And she meant it. Bedazzle. To impress with great brilliance.

Harper could be in a good mood, a bad one, pissy, upset, or amazingly happy for no reason at all. If she felt the need to share a compliment with someone, her mood was no reason to stop her. She would get the attention of the receiver. You bedazzle me. Or whatever her super-cool phrase was would come out. And no matter what kind of mood the recipient was in, she was immediately good. She bedazzled someone.

Harper did something beautiful with these strange compliments. She stepped out of a "you're so nice" box and into something unique. Something meaningful.

She told you something she thought was true about you in reference to her life. She knew sharing good was worth it. Even when she didn't feel up to it.

She was fun. There was never a dull moment with her around. But more than that, there was never a praise that went unsaid. If Harper thought it, she said it. In her uniqueness, she was able to demand the same kind of praise without requesting it. Because her differences called for attention to their kindness.

Harper lived well with others. I guess, we all would if we gave sincere compliments, regardless of how others may receive them.

May we compliment others in unique ways. May we find ourselves surrounded by those who bedazzle us. May we be so different that our uniqueness requires company— bedazzling alongside others. May we wear fancy pants. May we gift fancy pants. May we gift compliments in rare form. And regardless of moods, may we choose to say what others may need to hear.

46 SHAME KILLS & TRUTH SETS US FREE

Noah was a sweet boy. He was friendly, caring, considerate, and honest. He was scared. He was nice to the kids others overlooked. He had a great laugh. He enjoyed sports and movies, ice cream, and hockey games. He had kind eyes and an easy walk. He would do anything he was asked to do without question.

There once was a serious situation in the girls' house. A girl had taken some concoction of medication that had drifted over from the guys' house. If her friends had been honest with her (or actually knowledgable), she wouldn't have taken this medicine. A high was not going to come from an acne medication, a sleeping pill or two, some anti-malaria tablets, and an allergy pill.

This combination will not get you high and lifted. This combination may make one tired, cause a sensitivity to the sun, create some stomach upset, and maybe ensure your allergies are all in check.

But this particular girl, the one who was thinking she was set for the night, had an allergic reaction. She had to go to the hospital. She was not well. I knew pretty quickly from working so closely with the medicine where some of it came from. But I was bewildered about the one.

We questioned every single boy. Pretty quickly, I believed I knew who had snuck it in. I was so saddened. I believed it was Noah. And I couldn't believe it at the same time.

I talked with Noah. I asked him questions. He said he had no idea about the medicine. I no longer believed he had done it. I knew. I asked again. He still said it wasn't him. He was adamant. So was I.

We sent him back downstairs. We called up the other boys. They answered questions. We asked Noah to come back upstairs. I was absolutely sure. I was. I knew. He came up. We asked again. Still not him. I explained what happened again. I explained the girl had a bad reaction. It was serious. And although, it would make us very sad if it was Noah, it would not change the way we felt about him.

He looked up for the first time in the conversation. He breathed deeply. He started sobbing. He began to nod. It was his. He snuck it in from his last break. He never intended to hurt anybody. He really didn't. We knew he didn't intend to hurt anyone. Everyone knew that.

He was so ashamed. So scared. So sad. So disappointed in himself. He had done something he hadn't before. And a girl was in the hospital. But at the same time, he had admitted his fault. His wrongdoing. He said yes when it was so hard.

Although he was sad and crying, he was free. He was guilty but okay. He was disappointed but with something off his chest. He had amends to make, some consequences to own, some conversations to have, and some searching within himself to do. But he was free. He was able to breathe a little easier.

May we speak honestly when it's difficult. May we admit our fault. May we experience the freedom that comes from truth. May we separate from our shame and run toward freedom. May we, like Noah, trust that people will care for us even after we're honest.

47 HANGING WITH THE HOMELESS

So confident and comfortable with herself, a young lady named Heidi entered the program and my life. Heidi was beautiful and fun and loving. She was kind and funny, honest and loyal. She was easy-going and laid back. She didn't believe she needed help. She knew her parents would pull her from the program and bring her back home. How thankful I remain for their decision to do the opposite. How grateful I am to have walked alongside this young, sweet soul who finally realized a need for change.

Heidi enjoyed the high life. Literally. She didn't feel enough satisfaction with a high from weed. Instead she'd prefer to use harder drugs. And she found herself in the most dangerous of places. Getting high with the homeless. Under the bridge. In an alley. I hurt so badly as she told stories or remembered some of her fondest moments in the past few years. Mostly because she was too beautiful and naive to put herself in the places she did. But somehow, she remained safe.

To use a cliche correctly, Heidi has a heart of gold. She cares for every person she meets. The families in Haiti, the girls living in this house with her, the homeless man on the street, and family members that rejected or neglected her because of her choices.

After a long fight, Heidi began to hope for a change. She worked toward sobriety. She cared to fight for herself for maybe the first time ever. But what didn't change about Heidi during this transition was her ability and desire to love and help and change and grow.

Heidi would still find herself hanging out in the shadiest of places, offering the shirt off her back to the man without one. She would share a cigarette with someone asking for the same high she used to crave, knowing that high only lasts for a moment. And before you know it, the moment is gone, and the pain caused wasn't actually worth it.

Jesus is known for going to the lowliest places, being with the people without judgement and without fear, loving them for who they are, and calling them to a better place. If I ever saw this depiction lived out in real life . . . in this world, it was in this young, confident girl who found herself on these streets. A girl who didn't want help until she realized it was worth it.

May·we, like Heidi, love without fear and judgement. May we care boldly and without shame. May we go to the places that hurt in order to better ourselves and others. May we transition to lives of sobriety from whatever binds us from living life well.

48 BUT DID YOU KNOW I'D FAIL?

Kale was a awkwardly charming young man. He was funnier than most of the boys I knew in the house. He was serious about changing, but he was doing it for his parents, mostly, I think. He cared about the change himself, but it never was his idea. Kale did his time, so to speak, graduated, and left Shelterwood to go home.

Time went on. I didn't keep up with the boys. But after a while, I heard the news that Kale would be coming back. He'd done alright at home, but after getting in a little trouble, he had a couple of options and chose Shelterwood. It would have to look different, since so much had changed while he'd been gone.

This time, I worked in the guys' house, too. I had the pleasure of spending a little more time with Kale. He was still funny. This time, though, I learned his humor was to disguise his guilt. He had returned to a difficult place. A place no teenager wants to be. A place without parents but still with rules. A place without cell phones and facebook and driving. A place where freedom is earned . . . and the freedom gained never seems enough.

But Kale was grateful to be at Shelterwood instead of another place. So, he was respectful for the most part. We all get stuck. We all have ruts and rough patches. And Kale experienced that the second time around, too.

I left before Kale did the second time around. And I have no idea how his time there ended: in graduation, being pulled, or pulling himself. I only know that one day, sitting in the living room, we were talking about the first time he was there. It was a jovial conversation.

A lot was going on with Kale, and I wanted to be able to add a little life, a breathe of fresh air.

But did you know I would fail? I looked at him, puzzled. He repeated it. But did you know I'd fail? I still looked at him. Finally, I told him that he hadn't failed. 'But I had to come back.' Sure. He'd come back. However the changes he made were real. He went home. He lived better with his family. He had gotten into some trouble and had a few options. He chose to come back. I reminded him of this. Having to repeat something hard (and choosing Shelterwood is hard) doesn't mean failure occurred.

He was bewildered that I said this. It was like he was relieved. I'm sure others had told him he hadn't failed. But this time, he owned it. He hadn't failed. He'd gotten into some trouble and chose the hard road to getting out of it. He smiled a real smile, one I hadn't seen cross his face since the first time he was there.

May we choose difficult paths to get where we need to go. May we realize we didn't fail, if we're working toward betterment. May we allow someone to tell us we didn't fail when we forget. May we smile a real smile . . . especially we haven't in a while.

49 FREE INDEED

Joy was young and hurting. She was beautiful and aware. She was sad and confused. She was wounded and only knew to distract herself from the wounds by creating more. She was caring and deep. She was philosophical and witty. She was honest and scared. She was bold and daring. She was quiet, and she was screaming.

Joy longed so deeply for something she couldn't find. Something she couldn't attain. She was unaware that the wounds she carved were only deepening the pain. Because for a moment, for fifteen seconds or so, the pain was alleviated.

She found truth in quotes. She found solace in the redemptive part. The words that usually came after the comma. She wrote quotes she found on pictures she'd painted or drawn. She scribbled them on her body. She wrote them on the bodies of others.

When Joy first got to Shelterwood, she carved. She used the sharpness of a razor blade to cut away at the pain. She let the blood fall as proof that pain existed.

Today, she experiences something different. Today, she's free indeed. Today, she still has bad days. She still has to choose, every day, to do something constructive and helpful. To find solace in the quotes and words of others. To find truth in the part that comes after the comma. To work through the difficulty first to get to the redemption.

She knows that no smooth sailing ever made for a skilled sailor. She knows that without the rain, there would be no flowers. She knows that the moon still shines brightly even though it's surrounded by darkness.

Joy has chosen to overcome her own things. She's had a lot of people do this with her. She's accepted a lot of encouragement, hugs, tears, and prayers. She's allowed others to read and pray over and with her. She's yelled when she needed to.

Joy's graduation was the last one I attended at Shelterwood. It was my last day working there. It is probably the last graduation I will attend. All graduations at Shelterwood are beautiful and fulfilling and happy and full of hope. But this graduation, this celebration, this journey is one of the most beautiful journeys I've ever seen. And it continues.

She still uses quotes and song lyrics to explain her situations. She still is artsy and creative. She still has to choose freedom. She still has to be honest and bold. She still has to remember that before she graduated, she was . . . not okay. And that some days, she will still not be okay.

May we, like Joy, choose freedom. May we choose to overcome. May we hope for the part after the comma. May we go through the difficulty to reach the rainbow. May we, like the moon, shine brightly against and even amidst the darkness.

JAMAR ROGERS USES HIS VOICE & HIS WORDS

Jamar Rogers was a contestant on The Voice. He had an incredible talent and a moving story. He was invited to come to Shelterwood to share his abilities, his struggles, his triumphs.

We asked him to hold nothing back.

We asked him to share where he'd been.

And we asked to share how he had gotten out of that place.

If you are unfamiliar with this young man, I assure you, you're missing out. Please look him up on any social media site or buy his stuff on iTunes.

He did as we asked.

He shared. And he held nothing back.

The kids were so impressed by his victories. They clung to him. They sat and ate with him.

They asked him question after question.

They asked for his attention.

They shared their stories, and they held nothing back.

Jamar Rogers was so impressed.

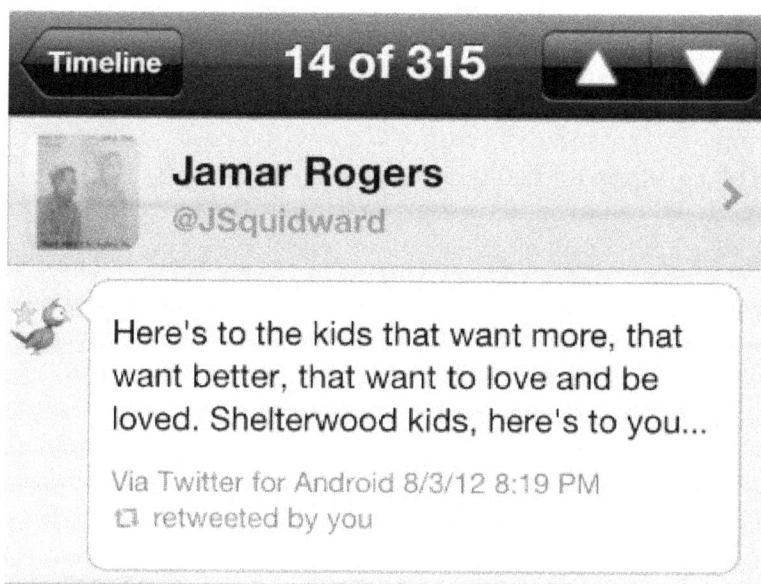

Jamar Rogers
@JSquidward

>

Here's to the kids that want more, that want better, that want to love and be loved. Shelterwood kids, here's to you...

Via Twitter for Android 8/3/12 8:19 PM
⟲ retweeted by you

The next two stories exist because Jamar came and invited others in.

50 WORDS CAN MOVE MOUNTAINS

Greg was sad and confused. He stayed on the fence. He wanted to impress people, and he wanted to be alone. He wanted to be cool, and he longed to be an outsider. He wanted to leader, and he struggled to follow. He was conflicted and unable to express what he felt exactly.

When Jamar Rogers came, he invited Greg to come play a song with him. Greg did. He grabbed a chair and his guitar, his humility and his humanity. He sat and played with Jamar (and Drew, Jamar's accompaniment) the most beautiful rendition of "How He Loves." They played. Jamar sang. And Greg was lost in a place of safety. A place where he faded and the music prevailed. The words and the sounds were bigger than Greg, and he was good.

Everyone was moved. People told Greg how well he'd done afterward, but it wasn't about that for him, and that was awesome. He didn't need the recognition. So much of his life was about recognition. That's what made this beautiful. Jamar was only at Shelterwood for the day. His presence was a great addition to the life and breadth and good that goes on there. When he left, the kids (and staff) talked about how cool he was and how great his story was.

Greg went back to his life of conflicted confusion. Jamar called me to thank me for inviting him. Really. We talked about his time at Shelterwood. We talked about some of the kids, the moments, the food, the pool party, about what had taken place: what we had a pleasure of being part of. We talked about Greg. Before we got off the phone, he told me he felt a need to send a message to Greg and asked if he could text it to me.

He did. I screen-shotted it (thank heavens for technology, huh). And I printed it. I gave it to Greg. He was so encouraged. He grinned. A literal grin. He was so happy. He was moved. He was changed. His confusion and conflict subsided. He was set for a little while. These words moved mountains for Greg.

He proudly posted them on his bulletin board above his desk. He would remember them as long as they were there. Hopefully, he still does.

May·we take with us our guitar, a chair, and our humility. Our humanity. May we play alongside those who invite us. May we be lost behind the words and the sounds. May we step out of conflicted confusion and relish in the words that call us to be encouraged and live well. May we post them above our desks. May we carry them in our hearts.

51 NOW, I'M FEELING SO HIGH

One of the songs that Jamar Rogers shared with the kids
was beautiful. The whole thing was great, but this song
particularly moving. It was sad and full of agony. It was a
confession that he was lost.

He sang, " . . . and do the only thing I've ever known to do.
So, I gotta, gotta, gotta get high. To kill my low. The
altitude's so high, I can barely breathe, but I don't mind at
all, because my problems can't reach. I feel so numb; I
feel so numb; I feel so numb. . . . "

He sang it boldly. It shared it graciously. He was honest,
and he was open. Eventually in the song, he gets to a
place of being saved. And he sings, "You take my hand
and say I'm better than this mess I call a life. So, I'm
feeling, feeling, feeling so high . . . because you took my
low. The altitude's so high, but I don't need to breathe.
Just stay by my side and keep loving me . . . " He
continues, "I feel so alive, I feel so alive, I feel so alive; I
feel so alive."

The kids loved this song. I loved this song. The words
were powerful. Bailey, though, she knew this song.
She may not have known the words initially. She didn't
write it. She didn't own the rights to it. She didn't
formulate the chorus or the hook, but she knew the song.
It was her song.

She'd sang it in some form for quite a while. After hearing
it, though, she learned it. She played it. She sang it. With
conviction. With honesty. With troubled eyes, a weary
soul and bandaged, but healing arms. "Oh, I
thought about suicide . . . I thought about ending my life.
But we're still here . . . the fact is . . . we're still here." She

kept her eyes down until the end. She played harshly with the guitar until the end.

And then she cried. No tears fell. But she cried. Just like the man who had written the song. Because the song was Bailey's, too. I feel so alive; I feel so alive; I feel so alive; I feel so alive . . . I . . . . feel . . . . alive . . . "

And she did. For the first time in far too long. Bailey didn't want to be so high in order to kill her low. Her low had subsided for the moment. She felt alive. She connected with the song. She knew the words before they existed. They were her cry already.

Thankfully, Jamar shared a story with Bailey who shared it with Hannah and me. And now, I share it with you.

May·we share stories. May we cry boldly. May we with troubled eyes, weary souls, and healing hearts go to the place where we feel alive.

52 HARD WORK U/Elaine

I went to a work-study college. Every person who attended this college worked for their tuition. It was dubbed "Hard Work U." It still is. I grew up with very hard working parents. They taught me about hard work, and I am so thankful. I've had a job since I was fifteen.

But I didn't know what hard work was until I met Elaine.

Elaine busted it no matter what job she was doing. Cleaning vans, the kitchen, her room, the showers, picking up trash, work hours, you name it. If you wanted a job well done, you asked Elaine. She wasn't looking for approval, recognition, or payment (although she'd gladly take any), but instead she was looking to give what she had in a way that she could. I told her once, that she put a lot of the Bigs to shame when it came to work ethic. She put me to shame.

It was from Elaine that I learned our work ethic goes with us and often precedes us. People usually know about how we'll work for them before we get there. Elaine was an example I wanted to follow.

Elaine was someone I wanted to be like.

I wanted to work hard enough that three years later someone would write about it. That someone would tell every person she did a staffing (semi-like an evaluation for the Littles) with about how our work ethic goes with us and often before us. That someone would encourage older people to work like me.

Elaine was that for me. I urged others to work like Elaine. To care about a finished product like Elaine. To know that what you do has your name on it whether you sign it or not . . . like Elaine.

It didn't matter what level she was or if she was working off consequences. It didn't matter if her friends were with her or if she was alone. Elaine worked the same for every project and every Big. She was consistent and helpful and good. She worked like she was born to do it.

And maybe we are. Born to work. Born to make a living. To do well and be proud of what pays the bills.

May·we work like Elaine. May we not care who's watching and work like we signed our name on the project. May we be consistent in our endeavors and know, without a doubt, that our work ethics go with us . . . and often precede us.

53 OVERCOME THE DEMONS WITH A THING CALLED LOVE

Derek was well-liked, charming, fun, and seemingly confident. What I learned about Derek as I got to know him a little better is that he wasn't so confident. He wanted to be, but for some reason, he wasn't completely sure of himself.

He liked and trusted me quickly. He was willing to talk with me present. He yearned to be known. He was afraid, of course, but he yearned deeply for someone to know him. I asked him to write me a list of ninety-nine things he wanted to do in his lifetime. He was so intrigued by this task, and he did it. He was becoming known.

I like crafty things, and Derek knew this. He asked me to make him something. I thought about what to do. I painted a canvas blue. Underneath the paint, I'd glued lyrics by Bob Marley. Overcome the demons with a thing called love.

It wasn't anything super superb, but Derek said he loved it. His eyes said otherwise. I began to question why his words and face didn't match. He said he did love it; he was just confused. I asked about the confusion. "Do you really think I have demons?"

I told him no. I said that I believed we all have things are make life, loving, enjoying, and being more difficult. I believed we all have struggles, sins, and difficulties. Whatever you want to call these things, they sometimes make living normally harder. These things sometimes seem bigger, more triumphant, and stronger than other things that are more important to us. Sometimes, even the fear of these 'demons' drives us to a place of assuming they'll win.

My encouragement, with a little help from Bob Marley, was to overcome these things with love. To say no to struggles and demons and yes to love. To say nay to difficulties and yay to triumphs. To say 'I can beat you' to the thing inside of you that stares you in the eyes and challenges your very being.

Derek was smart. I think he got it. He at least liked that they were actually Bob Marley's words. He thanked me. His eyes changed. They matched his words. He wanted to overcome his demons. He wanted the thing called love.

Don't we all?

May·we say yes to triumphs (knowing that they come after the difficulties). May we look to kick the struggles hard and conquer even our biggest fears, doubts, demons, and beliefs that we can't. May we, like Derek, begin the journey to overcome our demons with a thing called love.

54 SIMPLY PUT = GRACE

We spent a week at Camp Barnabas together. Helen was fun, polite, crazy, enjoyable, and helpful. She loved her camper very well. The two of them got along so well. They wore matching boots and cut off jean shorts. They smiled and made peace signs for pictures.

They danced and swam. They colored and read. They participated in the parties and both flirted with boys. They were two of a kind. Two peas in a pod. They were dramatic. But somehow, they worked well together and didn't steal the thunder of the other.

The camper would run Helen around and show her off to any cute boy. Conversely, Helen did the same thing. The girls were ridiculous, but they were cute, so you couldn't really be mad. They loved the songs and the action and the sunsets. The pool and the food and the games. The community bathroom and dessert every day. They were so fun together.

One afternoon, Helen had an accident in the pool. It was hard to explain. I still don't know what happened, I just know she had to go to the hospital to make sure everything was okay. The camper was super worried. I was scared. Helen's Mom was concerned.

Helen was okay.

It was a difficult situation. We'll call it grace.

Helen returned from the hospital, and the next few days were just had the previous few had been. Two peas in a pod. As if nothing had ever happened.

Helen continued to care for her camper and loved her very well. The two of them still flirted with boys. They still got attention without asking for it. They still matched their boots and shorts and enjoyed their time together.

Helen's absence for the one night didn't phase the camper. She still loved Helen. When camp was over, her Mom came in. She pulled her over to Helen. "This is my counselor, Helen. She's my best friend! She is awesome!"

She meant it. We'll call it grace.

May·we go on without explanation when something is different for a while. May we trust others to do well for themselves while we continue on for the night. May we run to others and show off the other pea in our pod. And may we, when nothing else makes sense, call it grace.

55 LOYAL TO THE END

Frankie was a comedic gent. He was cordial and inviting. He was working to better himself without the intention of getting home. He didn't enjoy the relationship he had with his Father, and believed it couldn't and wouldn't improve. So, he continued to make progress in all the areas he could alone. This isn't the goal at Shelterwood, but everybody's journey looks different.

Frankie had more loyalty than any person I've ever met. He loved where he was from. He, in the middle of a conversation having nothing to do with his home state, would just look up and boldly proclaim, "California." Not knowing Frankie, the other person in the conversation would be confused. Knowing him, anyone else would nod and allow him to say "California" as many times as he needed.

Frankie didn't talk with his Mom often, which he hated. He wanted to live with her, to converse and be with her. When he had an emergency appendectomy, I went to visit him at the hospital. He was in so much pain. He was in the Disneyland of hospitals, though, so that helped. But what he really wanted was to talk with his Mom. We got permission from his counselor, and he made a short call to let her know he'd had surgery, was doing fine, and most of all, that he missed her.

One time, we'd gotten wind that some kids were smoking. I knew that Frankie knew who the people were, where the stuff had come from, and when it was happening. I talked with him. He assured me he did know all of those things. He also assured me that he was loyal to his friends, even to people who weren't his friends. He made sure to let me know that if it was about him, he'd respond. But if pertained to anyone else, he was loyal to the knowledge and the people. Although he respected me and wanted to help me, he couldn't, because he valued his loyalty.

I told him that he would be helping them journey on and move forward. I told him it wasn't a coy to get others in trouble, but really to help them. He wouldn't budge. He said he understood what I was trying to say. He believed I wasn't trying to get people in trouble, but he still couldn't help me. So, what he could do was this. He would talk with the people. He would tell them what I'd told him. They could come forward if they desired.

I hated that he was withholding information. He said he had to. Withhold information to remain loyal. Loyal to California. Loyal to his Mom. Loyal to his friends and the information he had obtained. Eventually, we found out where everything came from. Partly because Frankie had talked with the kids.

May·we respect ourselves enough to care about our loyalty. May we respect others enough to remain loyal. May we give helpful information (and only if it's actually helpful), knowing that we can remain loyal by letting the persons know what we're doing ahead of time. May we, like Frankie, work toward things that are important to us . . . loyally.

56 I MISS YOU ALREADY

Vivian was a very confident girl. She had all the friends and enemies she wanted. She chose who she would let in. She could be so nice. And she could be so mean. Catty. Rude. But that was usually an act. She was caring, loyal, and true. Her friends meant the world to her.

Vivian was well-cared for and adored heavily by her parents. She didn't always know what to do with this love. It didn't always feel like it belonged to her. But it did. Her parents would do anything for her. They did. They did everything for her. She had anything she wanted.

When the kids went home for breaks, the Bigs would drive them the airport, wait with them until they boarded the plane, and call the parents to let them know the plane had left when it left the ground. This was not true for Vivian. She had a driver. Vivian left the property in a limousine. Or a very fancy black car. She packed her bags. She waited in the living room. The driver came inside, got her bags, opened the doors for her, and drove her to the plane.

Right before she'd leave, she got her phone for the trip home. All of the kids (who had them) got their phones when they left.

Vivian was being driven away in this beautiful black car to go home. And she has no one watching her. And she uses her shiny, sparkly phone.

I miss you guys already.

She's not even off of the property yet, and she misses us already. Because when you live in a house full of girls, you can't help but feel loved. You can't help but become close. You can't hide who are, and let people know you.

The prettiest and ugliest moments. You can only act for so long, before the person you are is the person who shows. It's one of the most beautiful things about the set up of Shelterwood.

You can't hide. And when we're loved for who we are-- even when we don't feel deserving, we already miss it as soon as we drive away.

May·we share with those that we miss, that we miss them already. May we be real with one another, and on our ugliest days, in our ugliest moments, may we know that being ourselves completely without disguise allows us to be loved well and wholly.

57 SHUT UP SO BRITTANY WON'T LEAVE

I had the privilege of attending group counseling with some of the boys a couple of times. The first time I went, I was so upset with how the boys interrupted one another. How the didn't listen. How the lay down and didn't pay attention. I'm not a big deal, by any means, but some of these boys really enjoyed my company.

So, when I was asked to come back, I agreed, although I hadn't completely liked my first experience. I sat down. The boys were rowdy. They'd just finished school, and they were only one hour away from freedom. They lay down and were laughing and chatting. They saw me and hooped and hollered my name.

I sat silently on the floor, my legs crossed like a Kindergartener. I cleared my throat. They listened. "This is serious. This is group counseling. This is important. It doesn't matter that I'm here, but I will leave if you aren't respectful to one another, if you lay around, or if you interrupt. I don't care if you need to sit on the floor like me, cool. If you're grown enough to sit politely and not be rude another, stay where you are. Ready?"

They sat. Stunned. No one had ever told them they'd leave if they acted out. They always acted out. But I just said I'd leave. I didn't know how they'd respond. In fact, I figured they wouldn't care. But Mason, he cared. "Shut up, so Brittany won't leave!"

Well . . . that wasn't exactly what I was going for. But they did listen. They were respectful. They listened to the kids they usually ignored. They gave feedback. I asked each of them questions, and they answered. It was a beautiful group. I took notes, and I gave them to the boys during the week.

If the group seemed to be nearing a rowdiness, Mason again would yell, "Shut up, so Brittany won't leave." Finally, I told Mason he could be a little more cautious with his words. But he really believed he was being respectful. He was making sure I was respected. I had listed a couple of things I wouldn't put up with. He was ensuring those things stayed away.

I didn't go back to group after that session. I didn't need to. They'd learned a way. They found voices. They were able to be respectful, and they saw importance in being so. They continued to listen to one another and care. They offered feedback. I didn't do anything spectacular. I got one boy to speak up for and with me.

And the rest listened.

Even when I wasn't there.

May we, like Mason, call others and ourselves to a place of respect. A place of listening and offering sound advice. May we stand up for what we believe in and listen as those we trust direct us to better uses of words. May we not shut up so Brittany won't leave, but instead . . . may we quiet ourselves and listen so that others will stay.

Marley was beautiful. She was soft spoken. She was humble and creative. She was incredibly caring. She was hurting inside and had been for a long time. She was ready and willing, though, to address some issues she never really had.

She worked so hard to overcome these stories from previous years and wounds that held her in bondage. Marley talked with those she trusted. She wanted to experience something other than pain and suffering. She wanted to be free from the thoughts and memories that held her captive.

She longed to forget so many things, but her scars were reminders no matter what she did. They marked memories that hurt; they represented the internal scars. These scars were visible representations that Marley was bound by things beyond her control.

Thankfully, she was honest. She didn't want these things to rule over her anymore. The hard truth is things only rule over us if we give them power. And so Marley took the power back. It was her's now.

The scars remained. They always will.

The memories of what they represent may surface, and again, Marley will have to remember she is the one in control. Things, memories, and people can only hold us down if we give them the upper hand. IIf we let them call the shots. Things can only win if we don't fight. And sometimes, the fight may not feel worth it.

I wish you could ask Marley if the fight is worth it.

Marley has overcome memories and scars that no one should have to experience. She has become *stronger than the scars*. She has found freedom. She has shown the visible marks that they no longer prevail. She has begun to sing and to fly. To be free. To taste the freedom she longed for.

May·we taste the freedom. May we tell our scars they aren't winning anymore. May we unlock the cage and fly away. May we sing and find shelter in the freedom that comes from being released into the world instead of hiding within ourselves. May our roots be deep like the tree you're about to see . . . and may we, like Marley and the bird, fly freely.

59 THIS IS NOT THE END

Penny came to Shelterwood with a journal in hand. She was always writing. She was petite and withdrawn. She talked with others and laughed, but she was seemingly alone. She stayed to herself and the journal most of the time. She was cute and fun. She was easy to talk with. She was willing to be honest about herself, but she didn't give too much.

It didn't matter where she was: church, school, the living room, her bedroom, in the car, or wherever. Penny had this pen and paper in hand, like it was part of her. Like it completed her.

I asked her what she wrote, and she just looked up at me, with the pen in her mouth. Nothing, she said. I sat next to her a couple times. It was obvious she wasn't writing nothing. She was diligent. She wrote quickly. I glanced over. She was writing a story. She was writing a story I'd read before.

To Write Love On Her Arms. The story of how that movement began. The story of Renee. The story that started with a girl who was refused at a rehab, because they couldn't handle her. Because they considered her too high-risk. A story that becomes beautiful. A story that shows what the church looks like. A story of a group of friends creating a rehab for Renee. Taking her to concerts and giving her cigarettes and music and coffee instead of cocaine and razorblades. A story where Renee is surrounded by people who care.

A story where a group of people long to write love on her arms. Where they long to write love instead of "Fuck Up," which is the last thing Renee carved into her arm.

Penny is writing this story. Word for word. She has memorized this story. It resonates with her. She has claimed the story. She has known the story. She has lived the story. And she longs for the rehab. The people. To love to be written on her arms.

I realized every time I saw her writing and was able to catch a glimpse of it, it always was this story. She wrote it everyday. She longed for it every day. Every single day.

She scratched the same two words, like Renee, into her skin. She continued to write the story. She continued to hope for redemption and care like Renee had found it. TWLOHA is a movement that started with Renee. Renee had to allow them to walk alongside her. And she, too, had to walk. The movement hasn't stopped. And we know Renee is doing well, but her story hasn't ended.

I think that's what it was for Penny. She wanted to know how it ended. How Renee ends up. How she will end up.

May we write a story of hope. May we find stories we resonate with. May we look for a people group who will love and care for us. May we long for redemption and beautification. May we know, though, that the rehab won't work if we don't work, too. May we live in the moment, in the minutes, in the current story.

WHAT I CONTINUE TO LEARN

If I'm honest, nearly every story in this book shares a lesson of either or. Either love. Or freedom. Several of them do intertwine. And of course, each child did teach me what I've written about. But more than anything, they taught me about love. About freedom. About redemption. About hope. And what it looks like to hope when it all feels hopeless.

Shelterwood is a unique term. A unique place. I'm thankful for Richard Beach, who also believed in love and freedom. Who answered a phone call from a dad who's daughter was struggling. Richard was mentoring some post college aged young adults when he got the call. One was willing to mentor the young girl. One was willing to counsel. And that's all it took: willing people to walk alongside. Shelterwood.

The word 'shelterwood' actually refers to a technique in growing trees. This is a technique that allows a smaller, less mature tree (one without the capability to be exposed fully to the sun) to grow under the shade of a larger, more mature tree until it's able to grow on its own.

This book is about freedom and love, because that's what all of life is about. It's what we are all searching for. It's what friendship is about. It's what the story of the cross offers. It's what I long for. What you long for. It's what we need.

Freedom.
And love.

Freedom in love. I wish it for you. And for me.

I've gone back and read the words in this book.
I've corrected several errors. I have taken some
pages out. And I have added some.

I am continually tempted to go back again. And
then another time, just to make sure that all the
errors are gone. That all the formatting matches.
That all the mistakes are wiped clean.

Then, I remember that this whole book, every story
in it, began because of some errors or mistakes or
paths that maybe could have been avoided.

I'm not trying to get out of something or be lazy.
Even make a statement. I'm merely learning, that I
will continue to learn from those who have taught
me all I know.

From the mistakes and overcomings of those, of
you, and of myself.

May we, together, continue to grow and learn the
things we didn't learn in kindergarten.

And may we be so grateful to be doing so.

t ·h ·a ·n ·k · · ·y ·o ·u

To **Janice and Kevin Pate**: for being my parents and trusting me as I made decisions for the first time on my own. For choosing me. For loving me the best you can. For your support even now. For always believing I'd write a book; I hope this one makes you proud.

To **Rhonda**: for mentoring me and sharing your life with me. For the coffee and food I'll never be able to pay back. For your couch. For allowing me to know your family. For driving me.

To **Jenny Lamar but now Ussack**: for holding me to high standards and doing the same for yourself. For being raw and living boldly. For your kind words and continual grace.

To **Ryan Frederick**: for caring so deep and wildly for your kids. For never giving up on them. For walking with me as I hoped to do the same. For counseling me without knowing. For giving the best of compliments to your Littles.

To **Sheri Nelson**: for being willing to help a new program become life-breathing and wholesome. For everything you gave. For your valiant efforts with the kids I loved. For speaking truth and sharing grace.

To **Joe and Darlene**: for your vulnerability.

To **RayLynn**: for your steadfastness. For your ability to drive real, true, raw statements home to the most un-desiring of hearts. For a walk on a trail.

To **Joani**: for having making the transition. For teaching restraint training and showing us the most neutral stances. For kids hiding under your desk. For allowing me to be a part of your difficult talks at Chick-fil-A.

To **Leah and Shannon**: for enforcing curfew. For the ice cream. For the bed you allowed us to use in to get some 'real sleep.' For adjusting to something completely different than what you'd known.

To **Jason and Tim**: for being willing.

To **Brad Edgar**: for being so real. Unashamed. For being helpful.

To **Luis Moctezuma**: for games of dominos and QT runs. For talks in the hall and for working hard to better yourself, while setting an example for the kids and for me.

To **John and Jane**: for offering your home and support time and time again.

To **Dena**: for caring for the kids as much as you cared for S.

To **Tracy White**: for caring so deeply. For the journal. For the prayers. For the love. For Easter in Kansas and New Year's in Kentucky. For letting me know you deeply and doing the same for me. For being honest. For your rawness.

To **Nancy Pants**: for days off. For the wisdom you bestowed upon me and the tears you cried with and for me. For walking through a new journey. For Starbucks and Chipotle. For the Leiboults'. For watching every Scarlet takes a tumble video with me. For the song that stayed in the trunk except when it needed to come out. For knowing when I needed to laugh.

To **Gail**: for stretching me. For calling me to good intentions and real conversation.

To **Stefanie**: for loving me. For accountability. For hope. For your honesty and love.

To **Vered**: for your Hebrew prayers. For your hugs. For apples and honey. For "Dare You To Move." For your willingness to leave a country you loved to serve those you did not know.

To **Marcedes**: for tea time. For tea. For the strength you brought, when you felt so weak.

To **Nate·Rayburn**: for doing it. For sticking it out. For walking with me in it. For singing over me. For loving the hardest to love.

To **Chris**: for your honesty. For the way you love and seay Nancy. For your apologies. For your hard work the years after.

To **Larry**: for your continued faith. For your love for Martin Luther. For your go-to statement, "Apart from Christ . . . . " For living the life you said you lived. For practicing what you preached.

To **Dusty**: for your laughter. For stepping out of your comfort zone.

To **Joni·RC**: for sharing with me one of the most precious people you know. For the text messages when you were worried. For the coke zero. For inviting me to stay with you guys when you went to a football game. For allowing me to stay the night before Christmas Eve. For caring deeply and making hard decisions. For never giving up.

To **Abby·With·a·Baby**: for all the encouragement. For your help, love, and wisdom through this process.

To **Frenzy**: for the haircut. For the encouragement. For the fight you fought a few hundred miles away from me. For the letters you wrote. For the honesty you shared. For trusting me even though I was leaving. For the purple bow. For more than you'll ever realize. Really.

To **Heather Norris**: for being the hardest worker I've ever known. For your attention to detail. For your love for the kids and the kitchen. For your integrity. For your willingness to stay true to the mission when the task was hard.

To **Matt, Kyla, Micah, and Tucker**: for loving me in the most amazing way. For gathering me into your arms and calling me home. For the birthday flowers. For the prayers. For the colored pages. For the meals before group. For the tears and wisdom. For the way you raise your children. For the behind-the-scenes things you did, even for me. For your family . . . becoming mine.

To **Finn**: Thank you for coming later. :)

To **Jackson Tefertiller**: for your humor. For speaking bolding into the lives of teens . . . and me. For working tirelessly.

To **Michelle, Jason, and Will**: for sharing your family. For french fries after serve days. For little art projects. For loving me.

To **Amber Thomas**: for fighting the good fight. For loving hard alongside me. For not giving up. For staffings that could have not existed. For pushing and pushing and pushing. For loving until it hurt and then loving more.

To **Jeremy Lotz**: for your patience and grace. For your ability to be in tune. For your prayers. For sharing your wife. For the occasional mountain dew. For the small prayer group. For hosting Jamar Rogers.

To **Jamar Rogers**: for loving Shelterwood. For answering an email and tweet. For being willing. For singing. For talking with the kids. For sharing your story. For your hope. For your love. For your belief in greater things to come. For your fight amidst your own hardship.

For your call to thank me for inviting you. For the text message you sent to one of the kids. For the lives you helped change and the ones to come.

To **Todd Ellett**: for the prayers requesting hedges of protection. For believing whole-heartedly in lives being changed. For believing in me.

To **Tacuma**: for your service. For showing the kids. For your kitchen class. For your hospitality.

To **Amy Sperle**: for your work. For naming the kids. For your love for the girls and willingness to stay up and fight with me. For your honesty. For your second mile attitude. For seeing me fall gracefully. For your help. For wearing the jumpsuit with me and another. For your friendship. For a trip to Florida and Ride Nature. For so much more.

To **Sara Jane**: for your willingness to go beyond. For caring for me during tough times. For your ability to dig deep. For crying in front of me. For laughing with me.

To **Meredith**: for quesadillas. For long talks and hard work. For that ugly painting we hung. For covering for me. For loving me. For not waking me up even when I asked you.

To **Amber Allen**: for allowing me so much grace. For being real. For loving alongside and growing with me.

To **Maggie (Smagrumieaux)**: for being real. For caring. For housing some of my things after I left. For working hard. For your hands. For soft skin. For Chipotle runs and Dominos pizza. For popcorn in colanders and texts from last night or dear blank please. For listening or falling asleep to my stories. For your bathroom. For kindly explaining hippa to me. For your friendship. For the chips. For your willingness. For your abilities. For your love.

To **Becca and Justin**: for your steadfastness. For your help. For your willingness. For your desire to step up.

To **Brian Albright**: for your counsel. For The Killer B's. For allowing me to know you and your family well.

To **Emily Sjogren**: for taking the high road. For staying. For allowing me to know you. For real talks and sweet notes. For letting me read your books.

To **Kamilah**: for being honest. For allowing me to love you. For your care. For your story. For your desire to love and be well.

To **Brooke Jacks**: for doing it. For running the race with perseverance. For allowing me to talk on the phone to your friends. For learning about and caring for yourself.

To **Courtney Gibson**: for more than you'll ever know. For loving me and allowing me to know you in a deeper level than I anticipated you would. For being real. For showing me what Christ looks like in a woman after his heart.

To **Dan and Jackie Cox**: for allowing me to be a part of your wedding. For trusting my decorating and throwing together abilities. For caring so well for one another and the kids. For showing everyone what love looks like in the midst of living under a microscope.

To **Daniel Schlenker**: for caring so well. For running a good race. For bacon. And guacamole. For taking care of yourself. For calming the kids. For attending group counseling sessions with me. For being a good friend to all you befriended.

To **Sydney**: for the run at the plaza to see the bachelor. For good talks and sharing life with me.

To **Hannah**: for laughs. For Eminem. For the ride to the airport to pick up Jamar and Drew. For wearing yellow and calming me.

To **Audra**: for your clothes. For your ability to care deeply. For your smile. For your desire to love and know well. For doing difficult jobs with a willing heart.

To **Kiley and Crystal**: for saving a life.

To **Julie**: for working hard with difficult kids. For being artsy and creative. For asking hard questions. For being bold.

To **Rujon**: for trusting me with a big job(s).

To **Stephen Hobson**: for teaching me. For trusting me. For officing next to me. For showing me that people pay for what they think you're worth. For answering my questions even after I left. For having a beautiful family with a beautiful story that I will cherish forever.

To **Jess McCay**: for trusting me even when it was difficult. For forgiveness. For grace.

To **Adam Hughes**.

To **Tom and Cindy Booth**: for everything. Literally, FOR EVERYTHING.

To **those not mentioned**: for all you did. For loving me. For walking alongside me. I am sorry to have missed your names; the list was far too long. I promise each of you taught me a lesson.

To **every little I spent time with**: Thank you in the most humble form.

To **the parents of the the kids**: Thank you for trusting me with your precious one. I am incredibly thankful and forever changed.

To **Rob Bell, Marshall Mathers, Jason Mraz, The Avett Brothers, and Bob Marley**: for wise words. For helping me tell stories. For telling your own stories. For being bold and honest. For truth. For recovery. You all have been so wonderful. Please take these compliments well, and don't sue.

To **T W L O H A**: for allowing me to share the story you've already shared. For caring well. For starting a movement and continuing it. For helping, loving, shaping, and saving so many kids I love.

To **Laura Edwards**: for a place to write. For a place to be safe and real. For the walk you took with me. For caring well, listening carefully, speaking boldly, allowing me to hurt and to heal.

To **Doug Starliper**: for the photo on cover and your willingness to be a part knowing nothing more than I liked wine and was writing a book. For meeting me in a park on a rainy day just because I asked.

To **you for buying the book**: I hope it's changed your life, your prospective, your view, your attitude . . . I hope it's bettered you . . . like it's bettered me.

May we all taste
and see the
goodness.